Fox

Animal
Series editor: Jonathan Burt

Already published

Crow
Boria Sax

Ant
Charlotte Sleigh

Tortoise
Peter Young

Cockroach
Marion Copeland

Dog
Susan McHugh

Oyster
Rebecca Stott

Bear
Robert E. Bieder

Rat
Jonathan Burt

Snake
Drake Stutesman

Parrot
Paul Carter

Bee
Claire Preston

Tiger
Susie Green

Whale
Joe Roman

Falcon
Helen Macdonald

Peacock
Christine E. Jackson

Fly
Steven Connor

Salmon
Peter Coates

Cat
Katharine M. Rogers

Forthcoming . . .

Crocodile
Richard Freeman

Duck
Victoria de Rijke

Cow
Hannah Velten

Moose
Kevin Jackson

Hare
Simon Carnell

Shark
Dean Crawford

Spider
Katja and Sergiusz Michalski

Pig
Brett Mizelle

Worm
Daniel Brass

Penguin
Stephen Martin

Rhinoceros
Kelly Enright

Fox

Martin Wallen

REAKTION BOOKS

Published by
REAKTION BOOKS LTD
33 Great Sutton Street
London EC1M 3JU, UK

www.reaktionbooks.co.uk

First published 2006

Printed and bound in Singapore by CS Graphics

British Library Cataloguing in Publication Data
Wallen, Martin
    Fox. – (Animal)
    1. Foxes 2. Human-animal relationships
    I.Title
    599.7'75

    ISBN-13: 9 781 86189 297 3
    ISBN-10: 1 86189 297 7

Contents

1 The Fox in Nature

The modern scientific names of the fox – distinguishing 21 species and 8 genera – depend on classical terms that refer to it as incomplete, false or ambiguous – or simply a bad creature. The South American small-eared fox, for example, bears the Greek tag *Atelocynus microtis*, which translates roughly as 'incomplete dog with small ears', and the *culpeo* – whose common name denotes its culpability – was once classified in the genus *Dusicyon*, which means something like 'a dog of bad character', but is now said to belong to the genus *Pseudalopex*, or 'false fox'. These aspersive classifications are caused, I think, by the fox's tendency to disrupt otherwise neat arrangements by its refusal to participate in a systematic account of nature, but also by an ancient tradition that considers the fox a wicked creature. The fox *seems* to be as open for study as any animal, but it is notorious for turning up where it had not been expected – or where it should not be – and for changing its defining qualities to adapt and take advantage of different situations. As common as the fox is throughout the world, it has mostly eluded scientific certainty, and the efforts of naturalists to rein in this ubiquitous yet elusive creature reveal the biases governing their attempts to define nature itself, which is equally elusive. Ultimately, to trace the ways that naturalists have defined the fox over the centuries is to glimpse the principles governing

Red fox (*Vulpes vulpes*).

different definitions of nature. The first Westerner to attempt a systematic account of nature was Aristotle, whose explanations may seem wholly unscientific today, founded as they are on beliefs that he took as truths but that have long been discounted. Nonetheless, his influence lies in the systematic approach he brought to classifying animals.

Aristotle follows three principles to classify animals: the different substances that make up analogous body parts; the different environments that animals inhabit – land, sea or air – which correspond directly to the substances of which their bodies are made; and the differences in their dispositions revealed through their interactions with other animals. Although Aristotle does not devote much space to foxes, he refers to them significantly in the explanations of his systematic classification, making them serve the ironically exemplary role of antipode to humans.

In the Aristotelian hierarchy, humans are closest to divinity, which is the pure life of light and air, and while humans do not quite attain divine purity, they do possess a fluid warmth. In Aristotle's scheme, the warm and fluid materials include blood, lard, semen and flesh. At the opposite end of the spectrum are the materials close to the cold, dark and hard earth, such as sinew, hair, bone, gristle and horn.[1] Man possesses the most complete body because his is the least earthy, including less bone or horn and more flesh and sensory organs than the bodies of other animals. Animals like the fox that are close to the earth are less complete, and therefore bony.[2]

In comparing body parts, Aristotle lays special emphasis on the genitals, because, in serving the function of generation, they most contain the nature of the individual's power of life. Thus his alignment of penises: 'The male organ shows much diversity. In some it consists of gristle and flesh, as in man; and the fleshy part does not become inflated, while the gristly part becomes

An Arctic fox cub in its den. Aristotle believed foxes to be colder and less 'complete' than other animals because they burrow in the earth.

enlarged. In some it is sinewy, as in the camel and the deer; in others, bony, as in the fox, the wolf, the marten.'[3] The three types of penises, those of men, ungulates and predators, are ranked according to what Aristotle believes they are made of. Since he sees the male human being as the complete form of animal life, foxes, in regard to their penises, stand two removes from the human and from completeness. A human's penis is made of 'gristle and flesh', while an ungulate's is 'sinewy'. Gristle and sinew are both earthy substances, so the significant difference here is that the human penis also contains flesh. Fox penises supposedly have neither flesh nor gristle-sinew, but are simply bone and therefore earthier, colder and less perfect than the penises of ungulates and humans.

The cooler and incomplete nature of the fox gains further elucidation when Aristotle describes the different modes of reproduction: 'The fox mounts the vixen for intercourse, and she brings forth as the bear does: the young are even more unarticulated . . . When the young have been born, by licking them

Red fox cubs. According to ancient authors, the cold, earth-dwelling fox could only become a complete animal when licked into shape.

with her tongue she warms them thoroughly and brings their concoction to completion.'[4] 'Concocting' in Aristotelean biology means completing the animal into its full form. This process, by no surprise, occurs through heat, so that, in licking her babies, the vixen warms them, shaping them towards the complete form, which is to be found in adult malehood. Foxes have a cooler, bonier physiology that is closer to the earth than that of humans, and so must be licked into shape.

The second basis on which Aristotle categorizes animals – their habitation – clarifies why he thinks of the fox as bony and cold, for an animal's habitat will determine the substance it is made of. Thus animals 'that are constituted out of wet matter are in wet places, while those out of dry matter are in the dry . . . The natures of their matter are of the same kind as the locality where they exist.'[5] What is more, he also says that animals' 'food differs chiefly according to the matter out of which they are constituted. For each one's growth comes naturally out of the same matter.'[6] Since foxes burrow in the earth, they would be made of earth, and would even eat that which they are made of, for 'what is natural is pleasant; and all pursue their natural pleasure'.[7] Aristotle's word for 'natural' here is *physin*, that complex term that may refer to origin, constitution and the physical element of which the animal is made. For the fox all these references coalesce, since it comes from the earth, is made of the earth and is cold like the earth.

With regard to the third basis of categorizing animals – their dispositions – Aristotle again ranks the fox towards the bottom – after the 'wild' wolf and the 'affectionate' dog – pointing out that the fox is 'wicked and villainous'. The Greek word that Aristotle uses for 'wicked' is *panourgos*, which describes those who hide in a particularly sneaky way, as Plato describes Socrates' foe, the sophist, doing, hiding 'in most rascally fashion . . . in a place we cannot explore'.[8] For Aristotle, then, the wickedness of the fox lies in its habit of concealing itself where empirical deliberation cannot penetrate. Again, because the fox lives in the earth, it is of the earth, hiding itself in darkness and cold materiality in a way that makes it inaccessible to empirical observation. For a systematic observer like Aristotle, an animal that conceals itself from plain view is wicked, since it represents the limit beyond which empirical observation cannot reach. In this way the fox again resembles the earth of which it is made and where it lives: the earth is too old to be known, and in the Greek view it is the realm of the most primordial and dangerous forces. The identification of the fox as wicked and belonging to some primordial chthonic order reverberates throughout descriptions and stories of all centuries and cultures: like the ancient and dark earth itself, the fox eludes the naturalist's best efforts at description because it conceals itself wickedly by hiding or putting on a disguise.

For Aristotle's successor Lucretius, who wrote in Rome in the first century BC, the 'nature' of animals retains the Greek understanding of what is revealed in the regularity of their actions, although he bypasses Aristotle's hierarchy of completeness by emphasizing behaviour over material constitution. The nature of a fox, he says, is to act as foxes have always done in order to survive through its ability to perform particular actions better than other animals can. Thus Lucretius departs from Aristotle by focusing on the non-physical characters of animals in order to examine the abilities enabling them to exploit their habitat. A fox will use its cunning intelligence because that attribute has saved it in the past, and so the fox can be defined as the animal with cunning. In this sense, then, the fox is neither more nor less than anything else (such as human beings), but is what it needs to be. 'Whatever animals you see feeding on the breath of life', Lucretius says, 'either their craft or bravery, aye or their swiftness

A red fox with its prey.

Four stills from a 1961 Russian film showing a fox feigning death in order to catch a crow. Many believe that the fox's willingness to deceive other animals is more than mere legend.

has protected and preserved their kind from the beginning of their being . . . First of all the fierce race of lions, that savage stock, their bravery has protected, foxes their cunning [*vulpis dolus*], and deer their fleet foot.'[9] Lucretius borrows the word he uses to characterize foxes, *dolus*, from the Greek; it may be translated as 'guile' or 'deceit', as well as 'cunning'. Like *panourgos*, *dolus* is a common description of the sophists – those false teachers who beguile people into thinking that the weaker argument appears the stronger; but the term is also associated with Aphrodite, who beguiles men, Sappho says, 'by weaving her wiles'.[10] In describing the fox as *dolus*, Lucretius recognizes it as a part of that natural power that aims primarily at deception; cunning guile becomes the governing element in the vulpine character because it has enabled foxes to survive for as long as there has been such an animal to feed 'on the breath of life'. But the fox's cunning is also the beguilement of Aphrodite, who charms rational men into allowing her to exploit them. Lucretius' *dolus* points to another quality continually associated

13

with the fox, namely its seemingly endless adaptability to any situation in which it finds itself.

Writing in the first century AD, Pliny the Elder, who probably had more influence on later naturalists than Lucretius, reverts to Aristotle's view that humans represent the completion of natural organization, and that the animal kingdom constitutes an inchoate human society with the different species similarly governed by the power relations of politics. Pliny thus introduces the fox in his description of the sympathies and antipathies that connect animals in 'certain kinds of warfare and friendships'. There are quarrels, he says, between different species, such as foxes and kites, and 'there is a small bird called the aesalon that breaks a raven's eggs, whose chicks are preyed upon by foxes, and it retaliates by pecking the fox-cubs and the vixen herself; when the ravens see this they come to their aid against the aesalon as against a common foe.'[11] Here the animals do not just prey on one another for food or territory, but

The Fox and the Stork, a water-colour drawing by Philippe Rousseau (1816–87).

because, like humans, they actively and consciously dislike one another. As an officer in the Roman army, Pliny colours his descriptions of animals with the martial tones of a warrior used to weighing up the friendships and conflicts that potential enemies and allies bring with them.

Through Pliny the Aristotelian scheme held sway for another 1,500 years, supporting the Judaeo-Christian division between humans and animals. Foxes received particular notice in the Christian era for residing in the earth, possessing an illegitimate intelligence for charm and concealment, and for being thieves; on these charges Christian doctrine identified them with the force of evil, as in the second-century text known as the *Physiologus*, or 'The Naturalist', where the fox is vigorously condemned as the Devil. Because of this religious bias, I shall treat the *Physiologus* more fully in the next chapter, but it is worth knowing in the context of natural history that this moral condemnation dominated the Western view of foxes until the Enlightenment at least. The Christian aspersion did not arise from the fox's ability to elude knowledge as it did for Aristotle, but from its association with the seductive power of the Devil.

Freed from religious bias, Enlightenment philosophers again took up the part of Aristotle's project that examined animals in themselves and through their interrelations. Further, with the age of exploration, Europeans began to encounter a broader range of animals, which revived questions of how habitat affects character. The Comte de Buffon, whose *Natural History, General and Particular* appeared in English translation in 1780, combines strategic elements from all three of his classical predecessors, describing animals in terms of their habitats, their relations with other animals and their possession of specific abilities. In this last regard particularly, Buffon aligns the animals in a class hierarchy, revealing the aristocrat's assumption that

American Cross Fox, 1845, hand-coloured lithograph by John James Audubon.

higher classes inherently possess more refined faculties than the lower ones.[12]

Buffon begins his account of the fox, therefore, as though he were differentiating human classes:

> The fox is famous for craftiness; and he merits, in some measure, the reputation he has acquired. What the wolf executes by force alone, the fox performs by address, and often with more success . . . He exerts more genius than motion, and all his resources are within himself. Acute as well as circumspect, ingenious, and patiently prudent, he diversifies his conduct, and always reserves some art for unforeseen accidents.[13]

For Buffon, the fox's 'craftiness' approaches the deliberation that Aristotle had allowed only for humans. In fact, in Buffon's account, the fox becomes something of an intellectual – a thief to be sure, but one to be admired for his genius. Indeed, in describing the fox as one whose 'resources are within himself', Buffon promotes Aristotle's incomplete and earthbound beast into a 'circumspect' intellectual.

Buffon also introduces the fox's habit of caching its uneaten prey, which not only supports the claim of vulpine intellect but also indicates that foxes do not hunt out of a hunger-driven necessity as the wolf does, but that they enjoy a bit of gentlemanly sport. And here Buffon makes a delightfully revealing comment: 'The wolf is not more noxious to the peasant, than the fox to the gentleman.' Thus Buffon aligns the two canids in an analogy of human class hierarchy: predators like the 'clownish and dastardly' wolf, which kill only to eat, are peasants, while the aristocratic fox hunts from an aesthetic appreciation for doing things well.[14]

Aesthetics also govern the decisions made by Buffon's fox about its abode: 'The choice of situation, the art of making and rendering a house commodious, and of concealing the avenues to it, imply a superior degree of sentiment.'[15] Buffon explains elsewhere that 'sentiment' is the quality of possessing sufficient cultivation to be capable of aesthetic judgement, a quality that makes the fox into the direct analogue of the human aristocrat.[16] And thus Buffon wholly subverts both the Aristotelian and the Christian condemnation of the fox as the wicked opposite of man.

Modern science has continued the Enlightenment attempt to establish universal standards of classification, reinforcing a polished version of the three principle bases of categorization established by Aristotle – physical structure, habitat and disposition. Foxes are no longer derided for being made of bone, but are classified according to skeletal measurements. They are no longer said to be made of the earth that makes up their habitat, but are

Grey fox skull from an 1850s *Mammals of North America*. Aristotle's belief that the bony appearance of foxes connects them with the earth is echoed in the way modern naturalists use fossilized bones to categorize species.

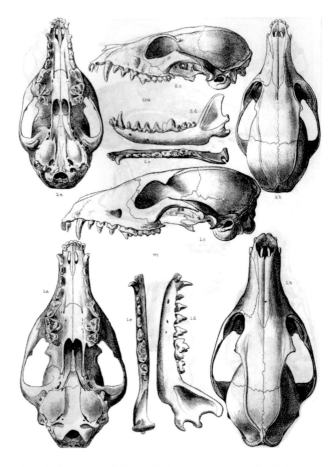

classified in terms of the kind of environment in which they are found – plains, woodlands, desert and so on – and in terms of their distribution throughout the world. Most importantly, instead of being called wicked for eluding empirical study (or said to possess an aesthetic sensibility), they are observed for family structure and for the schedules of their activity.

Contemporary science collects data from around the world on physical characteristics and on behavioural patterns, with the result that foxes are now said to be virtually ubiquitous, with the caveat that numerous animals of no relation whatsoever to the red fox are now officially designated 'fox'. How the different species spread throughout diverse environments provides the focus for much of modern scientific investigation, which is based to a large extent on fossils. Because the geological story of the fox follows that of changing climates and environment, its constant emphasis is on vulpine adaptability and on how the different species developed through access to new regions. This story thus provides a good introduction to the modern attempt to define the fox through a taxonomic distribution.

The geological record suggests that the spread of red foxes coincided with that of ice during the Pleistocene Age, and that the appearance of other foxes began with the retreat of the ice and with the geological events that bridged some land masses and isolated others. According to current palaeontological knowledge, the ancestors of the North American grey fox were

The grey fox of North America, the only species of fox that can climb trees.

probably the earliest foxes to appear, existing at least 3.5 million years ago; it was slightly larger than the modern grey fox with a narrower brain case. It probably lived in much the same habitat as the modern species – brushland, woodland and forest.[17] The modern species of grey fox has left fossil remains throughout the southern portion of the United States, extending no further north than Pennsylvania, and dating back 1.5 million years.

The progenitor of modern red fox species also appears to be the ancestor of the Arctic fox and so is given a name to suggest its relation to both *Vulpes* and *Alopex*: *Vulpes alopecoides*. Fossils in European sites suggest that this species first appeared around 3 million years ago, and was about the same size as the living Arctic fox, while its dental features resemble those of the living red fox.[18]

The oldest European fossils of living fox species belong to red foxes from about 230,000 years ago, during the period of glaciation from 230,000 to 100,000 years ago, when fossils show that red foxes became very abundant in Europe. Outside Europe fossils have been found from 230,000 to 400,000 years ago. The oldest American fossils of the red fox date from only slightly more than 100,000 years ago, indicating that it migrated to the New World sometime before that.

But while the red fox itself is a recent arrival in North America, its ancestors actually migrated from that continent to the Old World, as indicated by fossils in America that date back beyond 1.5 million years ago, exceeding the age of current European species by 1.25 million years. After migrating to Europe, the ancestral *Vulpes* became extinct in North America, then reappeared sometime between 300,000 and 230,000 years ago. In the far north of Alaska, *Vulpes* fossils have been found dating back to 230,000 years ago, but they have been found further south, from California to Colorado to Texas to Virginia, dating to 300,000 years ago. These vulpines are not

the direct ancestors of the red fox, however, but rather of the kit and swift foxes that in their current form live in desert and plains of the western United States. Evidence suggests that the range of these foxes shrank towards the north as the weather grew warmer at the close of the period of glaciation. Only recently have they expanded again in response to ecological conditions and through human influences.[19]

The kit fox inhabited North America long before the red fox immigrated to the continent.

In the South American continent canids in general appeared about four or five million years ago, when the Panamanian isthmus provided a land connection with North America. Fossils show that during the Pleistocene era the *culpeo* – largest of the South American foxes – lived all over the pampas. These and other South American foxes – in both fossilized and living form – hold only an obscure relation to foxes elsewhere in the world.

Remains of the living Arctic fox have not been found dating earlier than 100,000 years ago. These foxes only became common from 10,000 to 70,000 years ago, and, according to J. David Henry, are probably the youngest fox species in existence.[20]

Unlike other foxes, corsacs have round pupils and live in groups called corsac cities.

The *chilla*, like the *culpeo*, shows little fear of people. Charles Darwin famously walked up to one and killed it with his hammer – in the name of science.

What is notable, however, is that they seem at one time to have lived as far south as the French Riviera and even in Spain, indicating how far the glaciation spread.

The present-day corsac fox of Asia – one of the modern *Vulpes* species – may claim the oldest fossil records of any currently existing fox, since it had ancestors that differed only slightly from the living form dating back more than a million years ago. The exact relation of the fossil species *V. praecorsac* to the modern corsac, or to either the red or the Arctic fox, is not certain, however. Nonetheless, the prevailing view is that the living corsac resembles its fossilized ancestor sufficiently to claim a direct descent. Although there are older fossils than the *praecorsac*, none seems to hold such a close connection to a living species.

Geological records can provide evidence of an individual species' duration on the planet, and they lend credence to the existing taxonomies charting the relations among species distributed across the world. But these taxonomies depend entirely on anatomical details – which are all that fossils provide – such as skull shape and the number and size of the teeth. Henry suggests an alternative evolution, based on biochemical similarities and behavioural criteria, which not only maintains the relation between foxes and other canids, but also explains the similarities between foxes and cats. The conventional view has canids as one of three branches stemming off from the miacids, the small weaselly creatures of the Eocene (see the Evolution Charts). The felids constitute a later sub-branch from one of these three main branches, the viverrids, which includes hyenas as well as cats. Henry, basing his comments on the research of Alfredo Langguth, suggests that

foxes of the genus *Vulpes* differentiated early from the rest of Canidae and retained certain of the miacidlike characteristics – for example, a long tail, small foot pads, semi-retractile claws, and long vibrissae. While the rest of the Canidae family evolved differently, the foxes went on to evolve catlike hunting equipment in their morphologies and feline hunting strategies in their behavioral repertoires. This convergent evolution is expressed to varying degrees among fox species and may be most strongly expressed in the red fox.[21]

Henry's speculation provides an alternate narrative to the geological account of fox distribution, making ambiguity itself the defining quality of the animal that is the convergence of two separate evolutionary paths. From this perspective, recognizing the 'fox' in each of the 21 species requires the identification not of a singular essence but of a diverse and elusively fluid quality; the red fox remains the standard by which to measure other fox species only because it is the most ambiguous. Henry's account of fox ambiguity helps to make sense of how 21 widely different animals could come to be identified as 'fox'. If modern taxonomy recognizes the fox as an animal that can take 21 divergent forms, can exist in almost any habitat and manifests extremely different dispositions, then it has entirely overturned the Aristotelian need for distinct, unchanging characteristics. But the fox also causes problems for modern scientists who do not embrace its ambiguity as easily as Henry does, for since the nineteenth century naturalists have classified, de-classified and re-classified numerous canid species as foxes, expanding the genera of 'fox' to accommodate the divergences found among all the foxes of the world.

Starting in the late eighteenth century, as naturalists ventured outside Europe and met unfamiliar animals that were canid but clearly neither dogs nor wolves, they tried to fit these

A swift fox. Lewis and Clark recount seeing one outrun a deer when they were on their famous expedition to Oregon.

animals into the Linnaean taxonomy by referring to them as foxes. In using Latin and Greek names, Carolus Linnaeus created the taxonomy still used as a universal nomenclature by which naturalists might trace animal relations without being distracted by the plethora of regional names that usually involved some local legend. Consequently, the Linnaean system exchanged the folk and regional knowledge for a European perspective that identified the red fox as the standard measure for other foxes that sometimes hold almost no visible similarity to it. Thus the

European red fox is given the Latin name *Vulpes vulpes*, which simply means 'Fox fox', with the redundancy signifying that it is the true fox, and all other 'foxes' must approximate it in some way or another. The Arctic fox, locally known in Siberia as *isatis* and among the Eskimo as *Katúguliaguk*, was called by Linnaeas *Vulpus lagopus*, 'fox with a hare's foot', since it grows thick fur on the bottom of its feet to protect them from the Arctic ice. It has since been given the Greek name *Alopex lagopus*, to indicate how different it is from the red fox, since the two cannot breed. Although both *vulpes* and *alopex* literally mean 'fox', the use of names from two different classical languages reflects the modern effort to resolve foxy ambiguity by categorizing all its different manifestations.

The Latin *vulpes* was given to the red fox and the Greek *alopex* to the Arctic fox because these were the first species encountered by European naturalists, and so they got the names that simply

Arctic Fox, 1849–54, hand-coloured lithograph by John James Audubon.

A Darwin fox wearing a radio transmitter so that its movements can be tracked by zoologists.

mean 'fox'. But, when naturalists began trying to account for the animals encountered in other continents, they had to expand the meaning of 'fox' across species that vary so widely that they had to fall back eventually on the traditional recognition of the fox's character. No longer do modern naturalists overtly say that the fox is wicked or incomplete, but in their effort to arrange the nineteen species apart from red and Arctic foxes into a meaningful taxonomy, they have relied on Greek words that were originally epithets expressing the very same moral judgements that science has tried to get away from, for most of the terms do not literally mean 'fox' but serve as common descriptions of the fox's character.

A survey of fox genera (as they currently exist) on the one hand rehearses the geological narrative of worldwide distribution, and on the other surreptitiously reinstates the Aristotelian opinion that the fox is incomplete and wicked. The Northern

A bat-eared fox.

Hemisphere contains four genera: *Urocyon*, or the grey fox of North and Central America; *Fennecus*, or the fennec of North Africa; *Alopex*, or the Arctic fox; and *Vulpes*, which contains ten (or possibly thirteen) species. The South American foxes consist of three genera: the *Atelocynus microtis*, or small-eared fox; the *Cerdocyon thous*, or *carasissi* (crab-eating fox); and the *Pseudalopex*, which includes the *culpeo* and the *chilla*. Southern Africa contains a single genus, *Otocyon megalotis*, or bat-eared fox, consisting of a single species divided into two groups.

The North American grey fox was identified as a fox by European colonists because it looked like the animal they were accustomed to, except for its colour (although, in fact, the red fox often does appear in a grey pelage); but it actually does not hold any genetic resemblance to *V. vulpes*. The grey fox, which lives only in North and Central America, earns its own genus, *Urocyon*, a term coined from the Greek by the nineteenth-century naturalist S. F. Baird to mean 'tailed dog', since the grey fox is notable for the stiff bristly hairs along the top of its tail.[22] What Native Americans called the *colishé* does not even behave like a red fox in many ways: it climbs trees, lacks the strong foxy smell and, as the early twentieth-century naturalist Ernest

Thompson Seton put it, 'is less swift, less strong and less cunning than his cousin the Red Fox. The one is a bandit, the other a burglar.'[23] In other words, the *colishé* is not a fox – a *true* fox – except in its character as an unrepentant thief and its ambiguously non-canine trait of vertically slit pupils. The Europeans colonizing America looked for animals they could recognize, and, since red foxes were at that time rare in North America south of New England, the colonists saw the *colishé* as the New World equivalent to the vulpine thief they knew.

This same practice of categorizing unfamiliar animals on the basis of some, usually nebulous, quality of a familiar animal continued as Europeans encountered the species of South America. But at the same time, the names given to South American foxes reflect a real uncertainty as to how these animals resemble European foxes and even as to what they are as canids. Indeed, studies of South American foxes repeatedly stress that little or nothing is known of particular species, apart from the diminution of their numbers by fur traders or sheep ranchers. Three genera populate the southern continent – which has so far remained free of the red fox. The *Atelocynus microtis* is the single species of its genus, and in both its scientific and common names suggests no relation to European or Arctic foxes. Commonly known as the small-eared fox (*microtis* literally means 'small ear'), the scientific name of the genus, *Atelocynus*, translates from the Greek as incomplete or indeterminate dog. So this label tells us that the small-eared fox is not really a dog and its ears are uncharacteristic of a fox. Of course, the small-eared fox is 'incomplete' only because naturalists reject the terms of local descriptions, and measure it against what amounts to an Aristotelian standard of completeness.

Similarly, the genus of *Pseudalopex* is classified by the Greek word meaning 'false fox'. This genus contains four species, including the *culpeo* and *chilla*, that are notoriously unwary of humans: the common name of the *culpeo* refers to its folly in not knowing how to hide sufficiently to prevent it from being an easy target for hunters.[24] The *chilla* (*P. griseus*) is the fox that Charles Darwin killed by walking up and hitting it on the head when it was 'intently absorbed in watching' the activity of the *Beagle*'s crew.[25] Such un-vulpine foolishness convinced the Europeans that these foxes must be culpable and false – or, in a more Aristotelian sense, they, along with the *Atelocynus*, are incomplete and need further concoction.

The third and last South American genus represents the most extreme ambiguity in foxy classification – and perhaps even downright confusion. *Cerdocyon thous* possesses a single species, the crab-eating fox, known locally as *carasissi*. Its scientific name means 'fox-dog jackal', for, as Sheldon explains, the *carasissi* combines the 'characteristics of jackals, dogs and foxes in its social structure, life history and physical characteristics'.[26] The Greek word *kerdo* is one of the epithets that ancient authors used to describe the fox, but it primarily means 'thief'; so the 'fox-dog jackal' could also be understood as the 'thieving-dog jackal', and thus is a fox only because of its immorality and its ambiguous blurring of generic boundaries.

The effect of the effort at a universal taxonomy becomes most apparent with these South American 'foxes': among local people the *culpeo*, *chilla* and *carasissi* possess distinctive characters unassociated with the red fox: they are neither culpable nor false, nor are they failed members of other genera, but rather have developed relations with other animals and with people that remain unrecognized by modern science.

In contrast to the New World foxes, the best-known fox of Africa has retained its local name, fennec, as *Fennecus zerda*, a Latinized version of the Arabic word for 'fox' and the North

A fennec fox in sand dunes.

African variant on the Greek epithet *kerdo*. Possibly the reason is that Europeans long admired fennecs as exotic pets, because their small size (they are the smallest members of the family Canidae) and large ears make them decidedly cute. They have often caused a degree of doting silliness in otherwise serious naturalists, such as this from D. R. Rosevear: 'In many ways the little "desert foxes" reflect the manners of domestic dogs, as for example in their . . . turning around three or four times before settling down. They particularly resemble poodles in their ability to stand and walk upright on their hindlegs.'[27] Although they seldom weigh more than 2 kilograms, fennecs have been known to kill rabbits much larger than themselves, which is a point worth noting, since in the last two or three decades scientists have argued over whether they should be reclassified to reflect the fact that genetically they resemble wolves more than foxes. But here the reliance on ultra-empirical genotyping breaks down through the influence of the same Western bias that classified the South American genera as 'false' and 'incomplete'. The beguiling fennec remains a fox because of its charm and its ambiguous combination of qualities from both the canids and the felines: although genetically they may be wolves, and although they dance like poodles, fennecs have the most un-canine habit of purring.

Of all creatures, the fox seems to be the one whose most defining feature is its ambiguity. Even the standard species by which other foxes are measured, the common red fox, *Vulpes vulpes*, eludes definition through its variability. Modern natural histories emphasize that the red fox varies its diet widely and can adapt to almost any environment, precluding its identification with a single habitat. As we read about other species of fox, we often find that their ranges are limited by contact with *V. vulpes*, which adapts faster and to a wider variety of habitats than its cousins. Unlike many other fox species, the red fox is not listed as endangered anywhere – in fact, its spread has been a significant cause in the decline of other animals, both fox and non-fox species. 'The red fox's natural habitat', writes Erik Zimen, 'is the largest of all mammals, with the exception of the wolf. But the fox, not the wolf, has managed to survive over all

A red fox in beach brush.

his former range, in spite of extermination efforts and habitat destruction.'[28]

Scientists, such as Huw Glen Lloyd and E. D. Ables, point out that focused efforts in human communities to exterminate the red fox have had little success, and may even have somehow aided the increase of the fox population. Red foxes are the only mammalian species in Great Britain subjected to a 'Government approved and aided bounty'; and in North America several Midwestern and New England states 'have paid out millions of dollars in fox bounties' since the Second World War.[29] Zimen reports that of seven countries in central Europe, only two have closed hunting seasons for foxes.[30] But despite the bounties and unchecked hunting, the red foxes have spread throughout the entire northern hemisphere. They were introduced into Australia in 1845 for the sport of those colonists seeking to emulate English fox-hunters, and by 1893 had assumed such a strong hold on the continent that a bounty was established (further emulating the British). These invaders have contributed to the extinction of at least 20 native Australian species.[31]

Maintaining its ambiguous character, the red fox has adapted itself to the margins between human cities and the countryside; in fact, red foxes have become common within cities and suburbs. As human cultivation increasingly intrudes into wildernesses, the shyer species – such as the *colishé*, or the Arctic fox – disappear, and the red fox takes over. In our time, the red fox has come to symbolize the destruction of indigenous diversity and the colonial spread of European and American monoculture (and nomenclature). Consequently, even as a wild animal the red fox reminds us of what we would like to forget – that humans entering nature tend to change it irrevocably – and so the red fox's status as a member of nature remains among the most ambivalent.

One of the largest canids in South America, the *culpeo* is the fox that was known to the Inca.

Red foxes have proven so adaptable as to be common inhabitants of modern cities.

Although red foxes do not prey on humans, they do steal domestic animals, such as chickens and geese, and so natural historians continue to describe them in aspersive terms, as burglars and vermin, filthy intruders into a pristine ecology, representing an insidious threat waiting to exploit any defensive weakness. Indeed, much of the interest focusing on red foxes in the past few decades has arisen from the fear that they are contributing to the spread of rabies. This fear was the primary focus of a symposium in 1979 devoted entirely to the red fox, as noted by Zimen, who says that the heightened attention was not to 'the species itself, but its danger to human health through the spread of vulpine rabies over central Europe and North America'.[32] As a carrier of rabies, the red fox maintains its low status as an unclean animal, a pathological as well as a moral threat to human society and nature.

Zimen's comment lays bare another truth about the human attitude towards foxes of all the different species: even though they exist closely with humans, we still know very little about them. Aristotle complains that foxes elude deliberative study, and indeed they remain elusive, but the pathological aspersion has come to conceal that quality, enabling us to say that we do not care to know about them because they are thieves (*kerdo*) and unclean – in short, because they are vermin. And so the plethora of names – scientific and common – given to foxes around the world still reflects the ambivalence that humans feel towards an animal that is at once beguiling and offensive, charming and dirty.

Recently, two naturalists have worked to dispel the aspersions cast on red foxes. David Macdonald in England and J. D. Henry in Canada have each presented long-term field studies that emphasize the vulpine character more than measurements and distribution. Macdonald's work is among the most fascinating studies of any animal, consisting of a first-person narrative of living with foxes and allowing them to be themselves. Macdonald adopted a young red fox, Niff, which he made no serious effort to tame, letting her destroy his furniture. When Niff matured, he followed her to record her nocturnal jaunts in an up-close account free of moral bias that renews Lucretius' delight in the justness of the fox's existence.[33] Macdonald disarmingly observes that he finds the fox's scent pleasant, and then asserts that, contrary to common belief, the red fox 'is the least typical fox species'.[34] In stark contrast to the anthropocentrism dominating natural histories since Aristotle, Macdonald puts himself under Niff's tutelage: he describes how the fox taught him vulpine tracking skills, 'to pause as we rounded a bend or topped a rise, to see before being seen . . . My expertise as a tracker blossomed as Niff showed me each trick of her trade. And my trip through the looking glass was all the more exciting as her wonderland was so secret.'[35]

Similarly, even Henry's title – *Red Fox: The Catlike Canine* – embraces the ambiguity that most naturalists have tried to eliminate. Henry points out that although the red fox displays both the morphology and behaviour of Canidae, it also shares several features with cats, such as the long whiskers on both the muzzle and the wrist that serve as tactile receptors, the long thin canine teeth, the small toes and the foot pads covered in hair with semi-retractile claws. Like virtually all fox species, with the notable exception of the Asian corsac, red foxes have vertically slit pupils and along with cats they possess the *tapetum lucidem*, which 'causes the eyes of foxes and cats to occasionally glow a dull luminous green even though no strong light is shining into them . . . [and] acts like a mirror behind the retina so that light passes over the retina twice instead of once'.[36] In addition, all but a few species of foxes possess much smaller

stomachs than other canids, leading them to hide whatever prey they do not immediately eat among several caches; and foxes have demonstrated a strong memory of their hiding places.

Naturalists' descriptions of the fox uphold a consistency even through the expected differences of time and culture. From the beginning, the fox is said to be wicked, to possess an intelligence that is socially unacceptable no matter how charming it may appear.[37] Even with the rise of modern science, the accounts of the fox remain constant, which explains why the definition of 'fox' suddenly exploded into so many different species and genera in the nineteenth and twentieth centuries. Foxes possess a beguiling charm, but they also stink and steal; they remind us of our loyal dogs, but with their vertically slit eyes and their movements they are also like cats. They are mere animals, yet show disturbing signs of possessing an intelligence of forethought and

Red foxes display many of the same characteristics as felines, such as pouncing on their prey.

A silver fox.

aesthetic judgement that should belong only to humans. Definitions of 'fox' have tried to resolve the ambiguity surrounding the animal and the ambivalence people feel towards it, although the modern expansion of the fox into 21 widely diverse species reflects the fact that scientists still experience an unease towards the fox, since it precludes any singular definition that would identify it as a member of the ecosystem that performs a clear function that cannot be fulfilled by any other animal. Foxes have proved to be too adaptable, too variable, too elusive to be understood in the terms in which science wants to know animals. As Macdonald and Henry have proved, to enjoy the fox requires that a person delight in its ambiguity and elusiveness. The chapters that follow will attempt to do just that, and at the same time to show the different ways in which societies have tried to come to grips with an animal that disguises itself, keeps its identity hidden, has no sense of integrity and seems to have become almost ubiquitous.

2 Vulpine Myths, Folk Tales and Allegory

Despite its claims to objectivity, natural history cannot free itself from the cultural biases that hold the fox to be a wicked and cunning thief. This bias persists in the West because of a long history of folk tales and visual art depicting foxes in precisely these terms. In mythic systems from other parts of the world, the fox may guide a young person from one phase of life to another, or may change its physical appearance, and all the stories together cast the fox as the animal embodiment of nebulous and frightening forces akin to fire that emanates from the ancient earth. There are many animal stories around the world – especially children's stories – where the fox displays no particular characteristic distinct from any other animal. Some of these narratives simply provide explanations of natural details, as in the Russian fairy tale 'The Fox as Shepherd', which tells how the fox got the white tip on its tail. Consistent motifs do appear among cultures, however, for the fox embodies a primal force that can be helpful or malevolent; it is associated with fluid malleability; and it knows more about us than we do about it. And, although fox myths in the Andes and Arctic involve species other than *Vulpes*, almost all the other myths, folk tales and allegories refer to the one species of the red fox.

In ancient Greece the fox makes notable appearances in two forms, the first of which is the more startling and archaic, as

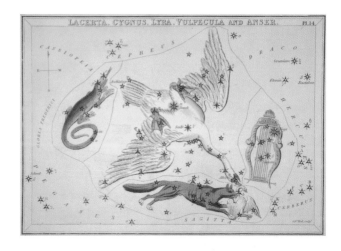

though it is a carry-over from some mythic system antedating the Greek. This is the Teumessian fox who sorely oppressed Thebes, as recounted by Apollodorus, Pausanias, Corinna and others. Offspring of the two serpents, Typhoeus and Echidna, the giant vixen lurked around the main road just outside Thebes eating the sons of the citizenry.[1] When the legendary hero Amphitryon was forced to flee his homeland, Tiryns, he found sanctuary among the Thebans, who hoped that he would help to free them from the Teumessian fox. Because the vixen was destined never to be caught, Amphitryon fetched from King Cephalus of Athens the famous dog Laelaps, who was destined to catch everything he chased.[2] In this version of the myth, Zeus resolved the conflict of contradictory fates by turning both animals into stone, making them into topographical landmarks and monuments of the racial history of Thebes.

This story reverberates throughout more famous Theban myths, for the Boeotian lyric poet Corinna claims that it was Oedipus who killed the Teumessian fox before he destroyed the

كوبت وزرك او وفاخره را واز باشد اكر خس است مارا اچنانكه مقام صوا ب باشد دست كفت
جو ابن اواز ملك را هيج رهبتى بو ده است كت نركت نشا بد كه ملك بدين موجب مقان و م
كرد ا ند وبكذا رد و وا وطنى با لوف محرت كند كه كه أنداقت عقل نقتين وا قف مروت جو مك وا
دل ضعيف او از بلند و ربعضى از امثال لالست كه هرا وازى بلند وجة قوى النغات نبا يد نمود
جو بن قصه روبا وطبل شر حكايت كت اورده اند كه روبا بى در بشة طبقى

سلوى در جستى افتاده و مركا كى با دمى بستى شاخ درخت بر طبل رسيدى اواز سهمنا ك و ش
روبا ه آمدى چون روبا ه ضخامت حب بد بد و مهابت و اواز مشنيد طمع در بست كه كوشت و بوست

'The Fox and the Drum', from *Kalila wa Dimna*, originally composed in Sanskrit c. 200 BC, and here illustrated in a mid-15th century Persian book of fables from Herat.

Sphinx. That she should combine the two myths suggests that the Teumessian fox served as a prototype for the Sphinx, which is generally regarded as a late import to Greek mythology from Egypt or Mesopotamia, and which was also born to Echidna. Analogously, Pausanius says that Dionysus created the Teumessian fox out of anger towards the Thebans for refusing to recognize his divinity.

At any rate, the Teumessian fox begins the Western vulpine tradition. She holds no overt similarity to later fox legends, except as a representation of a frightening power that must be contained and expelled in order for the community to survive. In this cultural context that associates foxes with such uncertain and primordial dangers, it is easy to understand Aristotle's moral condemnation. And between the Teumessian fox and Aristotle stands Aesop, who focuses the chthonic power lying in wait outside the city limits into the most famous characteristic of the fox – its intelligence, which is always described as working outside the publicly acceptable rationality.

In one of the most potent Aesopean fables, a leopard and a fox argue about who has the best looks. The leopard points to his coat and says that the fox has nothing to match it. In one twentieth-century translation, the exchange goes thus: 'The

'The Fox and the Lion', from a 15th-century Florentine manuscript whose Greek text copies a printed edition of Aesop's *Fables*.

leopard said, "Look at my smart coat; you have nothing to match that." But the fox replied, "Your coat may be smart, but my wits are smarter still."[3] In the Greek text Aesop's wit works through a pun: just as the leopard has a mottled coat, so the fox has a mottled mind. The crucial word is *poikilos*, which can refer to the leopard's spots as well as to the shimmer of a bronze weapon glittering in the sun; it carries the sense of iridescence, of a complexity of appearance that shifts and changes itself through a fluidity of form. So, the 'smartness' of the leopard's coat that is matched by the fox's 'smart' wits plays on the shifting, shimmering fluidity of the vulpine intelligence, which is commonly identified as cunning, the mental ability held in low regard for its shifty ability to subvert the proper – or at least expected – order of things. Cunning is represented in Greek myths by the goddess Metis, who for a while eluded Zeus' attempts to eat her by continually shifting shape and size, and

'The Fox and the Crow', from Jean de La Fontaine, *Fables*. A number of European folk-tales feature foxes and crows as rivals.

‘The German
Fox and the
British Lion’,
cartoon from
Punch, c. 1880s.

PUNCH, OR THE LONDON CHARIVARI.—November 17, 1888.

THE GERMAN FOX AND THE BRITISH LION.

Fox. "ACH! YOU EAT ZO NOPLE ARE—ZO SCHDRONG—ZO MACNÄNMISCH!—LET US IN ZIS ZO HOLY
GRUSADE TOGEZZER CHOIN! YA?"   The Lion. "HUMPH!!!"

who, once caught, provided the ruler of Olympus with a new
and subtle intelligence able to foresee the other gods' traps.

The shimmering iridescence of vulpine cunning enables
Aesop's fox, like the goddess Metis, to anticipate and delude
his opponents through numerous tales. In the most famous
story, for example, a fox sees a raven carrying a stolen cheese
in her beak. When the fox compliments the bird on her
plumage and wonders if her voice is equally beautiful, the
raven begins to sing, and, of course, the cheese falls from her
mouth. The fox steals what the bird has stolen, and leaves her
with the observation: 'you have a voice, madam, I see; what
you want is wits'.[4]

Several stories develop an extended warfare between the wolf and the fox. Always the wolf believes that the fox is absent and foolishly reveals his plans, unaware that his enemy is hidden in a nearby burrow. In one account, after losing his tail to vulpine connivance, the wolf seeks his revenge by telling the sick lion that he would find a definite cure in wrapping the fox's skin around his belly. But, lurking underground, the fox has overheard the wolf and covers himself in dung, to ensure that his skin would be too smelly for anyone else to wear. And, since the wolf does not stink, it is he who loses his skin to the sick lion king, compounding the earlier loss of his tail. The wolf repeatedly loses in these contests because he possesses no subtlety, no power apart from brute force, while the fox has the underground and anti-social intelligence of cunning, reviled for being immoral and sleazy, a mark of the coward and not the upright hero.

Moral condemnation of vulpine intelligence achieves its fullest development in the Christian tradition. The Christian fox first appears in *Physiologus*, a work from the second century AD that casts the fox as the Devil whose deceptions lead to hell. Just as the fox injures the earth by burrowing holes into it, *Physiologus* says, the Devil burrows into the human soul. The earth should bring forth fruits of righteousness, but once injured allows the grapes to wither, as reflected in the command from the Song of Solomon (2: 15): 'Bring me the little foxes, for they destroy the grapes'. The most common Christian story of vulpine deception is that of the fox playing dead to lure the

A fox feigns death in order to catch a bird, from an early 14th-century manuscript.

crow close enough that he may jump up and eat it. Like the Teumessian fox, the *Physiologus* fox emphasizes the predatory mercilessness of the animal; where the Greek myth presents the threat through the fox's giant size and its predilection for children, the Christian allegory reminds us that the Devil can never be made safe, and will attack us just when we think ourselves least vulnerable.[5] Christian tales simplify the fox's character, reducing the subterranean complexity of Greek cunning to mere deceit, and while the Christian fox grew in subtlety over time, it remained simply evil.

The identification of the fox with simple evil is corroborated in biblical texts, when Jesus, playing the role of Amphitryon, expresses his defiance to Herod by telling his listeners: 'Go and tell that fox, "Behold, I cast out demons"' (Luke 13: 32). Even if Luke had never heard of the Teumessian fox and of Amphitryon the heroic saviour, the connection between the fox and oppressive, elusive threats, along with the hope that someone will arrive to dispel the threat, had already clearly become enough of a motif that it could be applied to signify tersely that Herod is the un-catchable threat and Jesus the newly arrived hero. The fox and Herod both speak falsely to achieve their unjust aim of ruthless predation: 'The devil and the reprobate are crafty like the fox, and deserve shame. He who speaks fair words and meditates evil is a fox; such a one was Herod for he said that he would believe on Christ, when he really meant to kill him.'[6] As Herod plays false, so does the devil, and so does the fox. In these allegories the fox does not engage in entertaining escapades of outwitting his predatory opponents, but represents only the predator disguised as a trustworthy man – the preacher.

Thus the priest or preacher who lusts after his congregation is the vulpine Satan. A woodcarving in Ely Cathedral depicts a fox dressed in episcopal robes preaching to some geese from the

A fox preacher in stained glass in Ely Cathedral, Cambridgeshire.

A carving of a fox preacher in Wells Cathedral, Somerset.

text 'God is my witness how I long for you all in my stomach'.[7] Throughout the cathedrals of Europe this same scene of the devil-fox disguised as a priest about to devour the innocent unsuspecting members of a flock (or, less metaphorically, gaggle) is depicted in stained-glass windows and stone and wood carvings.[8] Indeed, according to Beryl Rowland, of all animals known in the Middle Ages, the fox 'was the most frequently used in art and architecture', for the appearance of the wicked fox naturalizes the belief in vulpine evil.[9] While other predators, such as the wolf and eagle, work in a straightforward, let us say honest, fashion that makes their violence seem acceptable, the fox works in disguise and casts his expressions of lust as prayers – 'how I long for you all in my stomach' – and he commits the two worst sins: he exploits the sanctity of priesthood to prey on innocent victims, and he disguises himself as a victim to seem vulnerable. The sexual connotation of the priestly disguise is reinforced by the depiction of the parish flock as geese, which appear innocent, if only because of their ignorant vulnerability. In preying on them, the fox becomes more than a natural predator, he is the satanic victimizer, the violator of innocence.

Out of this simple dichotomous morality of the *Physiologus* developed the great tradition of Reynard; indeed, the two strains of religious allegory and folklore often influenced one another, so that, for example, the misericord carvings of foxes throughout Europe depict many scenes from the Reynard stories but with the obvious intention of enacting Christian condemnation of sin. The narrative of Reynard, translated and published in English by William Caxton in 1481, consists of numerous adventures recognizable from Aesop, but, instead of devoting tales to different animals, *The Historye of Reynart the Fox* puts one character at the centre of everything – the fox that has too much fun making trouble for everyone else.

Caxton's tale opens 'about the time of Pentecost or Whitsuntide', when 'the lion, the noble king of all beasts, would in the holy days of this feast hold an open court at Stade'.[10] All the animals come except for Reynard, 'for he knew himself faulty and guilty in many things'. Naturally then, the others take the opportunity to complain 'sore on Reynard the fox'. Isengrim the wolf – Reynard's bitterest enemy, whom he has repeatedly cuckolded – is the first to complain, saying that Reynard caused the wolf children to go blind when he 'bepissed' them. Chanticleer the cock tells of how, disguised as a monk, the fox ate eleven of his unsuspecting chicks. Corbant the rook repeats the story from the *Physiologus*, telling of how his wife, Sharpbeck, approached the seemingly dead Reynard who jumped up and bit her head off.

It is only when the king sends Bruin the bear to fetch Reynard that we finally meet the fox himself in his castle, Maleperduys. Reynard 'had many a dwelling place, but the castle of Maleperduys was the best and fastest burg that he had. There lay he in when he had need and was in any dread or fear.' The reason this is Reynard's favourite castle is that

> Maleperduys was full of holes, here one hole and there another and yonder another, narrow, crooked, and long, with many ways to go out, which [Reynard] opened and shut after that he had need. When . . . he wist that any sought him for his misdeeds and trespasses, then he ran and hid from his enemies into his secret chambers that they could not find him, by which he deceived many a beast that sought him.[11]

Reynard's castle – whose name is taken from the abode of the contemporaneous epic hero Tristan – is a labyrinth, and the direct embodiment of the crooked, subterranean intelligence that enables the fox to elude his enemies and to anticipate their assaults. Even though the character of Reynard arose from the Christian system, and from the *Physiologus* in particular, he has returned to the more complicated Greek characterizations of elusive vulpine cunning.

Reynard's labyrinthine house shows why European folk tradition should develop the fox into a complex and entertaining character enduring for almost 900 years, while official Church doctrine confined the fox to the simple representation of evil. Bruin the bear – who forever stands as the plodding and straightforward dimwit in service to authority – epitomizes the attempts by legal and authoritative forces to contain and regulate what remains elusively fluid and subterranean. The elusiveness makes the fox dangerous to authority, since enforcers of the law do not know where to begin looking for him, and fear that he may be anywhere. Maleperduys represents the way that the fox is everywhere at once, and very possibly nowhere at all. The only way to engage with Reynard is to approach him on his own terms, to go underground and to give up any notion of dull ursine integrity. Reynard's multiple houses of many crooked passageways metonymically embody the vulpine ethos that does not belong to one place and which undermines the orderly world of social codes of allegiance and distinctions. Medieval Church and State authorities may have feared Reynard, but to the itinerant artisans working on the great cathedrals of Europe he clearly embodied the defiance they desired to throw in the face of their oppressors. As Donald Sands comments, 'it is possible to admire [Reynard], but in conventional circles we would perhaps hesitate to voice our admiration, for he is dangerously kin to our asocial selves'.[12]

As Caxton's tale continues, the fox's nephew, Grimbert the badger, convinces Reynard to return to court to face the charges against him. When Reynard appears before the lion, 'there was non so poor nor so feeble of kin and friends but that he made him ready for to complain on Reynard the fox'. Reynard is predictably sentenced to be hanged, for 'all his flattering words and deceits could not help him'.[13] This scene stands among those from the epic most commonly depicted in various illuminations, engravings and carvings, with the procession of animals creating a sense of festivity – both from the spectacle of a famous rogue being hanged and from the more pious aim of extricating Christian evil.

William Caxton translated *Reynard* into English from Middle Dutch around 1481, and the version he relied on, *Die hystorie van Rynaert die Vos*, itself derived from a verse epic written about 1375 entitled *Reinarts historie*. Medieval literary scholars have found fragmentary manuscripts of the Reynard story dating back to the first half of the fourteenth century, and these are taken to be copies of earlier manuscripts of an epic written down by an unknown scribe named Willem, who foxily burrowed his name into the final lines of the poem as an acrostic sometime before 1272. Three earlier beast epics involving the fox are known to have existed: *Reinhart Fuchs* is a Middle High German poem from around 1182; *Ysengrimus*, named for

A panel from an issue of Imbar and Hubert's *Le Polar de Renard*, a 20th-century re-telling of the medieval French *Roman de Renart* (c. 1175).

Reynard's arch-enemy, is a Latin poem from around 1150; and *Echasis captivi* ('The Production of the Idle Hours of a Captive'), also in Latin, appeared about 940.

My purpose in tracing this textual lineage is to point out the duration of the Reynard tradition in Europe. For almost 800 years, the fox provided a distinct mythos for literature, drama and ecclesiastical allegory in church sculptures, woodcarvings and stained glass. The individual representations of these scenes may be satirical and humorous, or grimly allegorical, depending on whether the poet, scribe or woodcarver saw the fox as entertainer or as allegory of Satan. The pliability of the fox in serving as both entertainment and instructional warning against evil made him enormously popular throughout Europe. In fact, in his discussion of Ben Jonson's play of 1601, *Volpone*, R. B. Parker asserts that 'the epic of Reynard the Fox was perhaps the most widely known story in medieval Europe'.[14]

Ingeniously, Jonson transformed the animals into humans who are recognizable as types because of their participation in the familiar portraits of venality and subterfuge. Volpone pretends to be on his deathbed so that Voltare, Corbaccio and Corvino – or Vulture, Raven and Crow – will try to bribe him into leaving his wealth to one of them. Volpone unabashedly deceives, cheats and cuckolds the crows, who hope to prey upon his carcass. Only at the end does his scheme collapse as his treachery is exposed in court. The contrivance of this ending provides a strong suggestion that Jonson relied less on literary sources – which consistently have the fox getting off altogether so that he may pursue more deceptions – than on the visual tradition of carvings and stained-glass windows, where the fox is often hanged. Indeed, Reynardiana was so widespread throughout Europe as to constitute a common knowledge, confining

Reynard Confessing from the Gallows, 1846, an etching by Wilhelm von Kaulbach.

Jonson to no one particular source. His true innovation was to cast the ever-present fox in human garb.[15]

In 1794, about 180 years after Jonson's play was first performed, Goethe published his *Reineke Fuchs*, which, in contrast to Christian warnings of satanic deceptions, attacks the German political scene, criticizing the arrogance and egotism of the aristocracy. Goethe identified with Reineke the fox, for, in the words of Roger Stephenson, 'Reineke's superiority over the other animals' consists not in being more clever, as is the case generally in the tradition of European fox tales, but in being better'.[16] Goethe purifies vulpine intelligence of its roguish displays in order to draw out the aloofness of the fox, which belongs to no society. In the Christian version, unsociability is another mark of vulpine evil, but, from the perspective of the fox, it is society that appears corrupt and the outsider free from sin.

While the foxes of other cultures do not always display the amorality of Reynard, they do situate themselves, like Goethe's outsider, along margins and boundaries. This placement, complemented by the association with primordial power, makes the fox into a vital and positive element in South American myth. Among the Andean Quechua, descendants of the Inca, the fox plays a transformational role among family relationships from its position between two territories or between two phases of life. Gary Urton explains how the ritual co-parenthood, or *compadrazgo*, common throughout the Andes today is an amalgamation of indigenous and Spanish family institutions. In the system of *compadrazgo* 'adults contract fictive or spiritual kinship through ritual sponsorship of a child or object'.[17] In these ritual kinships, the puma is referred to as either *Machu Compadre*, ancient male co-parent, or *Machu Comadre*, ancient female co-parent, to the newly born first son. The fox then takes the middle position as the son of *Machu Compadre* and therefore the father of the child. This family alignment not only provides protection for the infant, but facilitates the transition of the human parents into full members of the community. In bearing their child, the human parents, then, inherit the social formation that the community has modelled on its interactions with animals.

The fox as parent represents a crucial step in the transition from childhood to adulthood. Each year a young man is elected by the community to serve as guardian of the crops, who is known as *ararihua*, or the public announcer. He leaves home to reside by the fields, where he protects the crops from marauding foxes, and, when he returns home, the young man has changed from youth to adult. Usually he is already married and the father

A drawing of an *ararihua* (Quechua fox disciple), from Felipe Guaman Poma de Ayala's manuscript, *El primer nueva coronica y buen gobierna* (1583–1615).

of one or two small children, which puts him in the same position as the son of *Machu Compadre*, the fox. Chronicles from the time of the Inca depict the *ararihua* wearing fox skins over their shoulders with the fox's head on their own, indicating how the young man must become a fox of sorts in order to accomplish the important transition from youth to citizen.

Tom Zuidema says that the word *ararihua* derives from the Aymara term, *huararihuasita*, meaning 'to shout very much when people catch the fox or wolf who steals'.[18] The young guardian wears the skin and head of the animal he must protect the fields from, and in effect assumes the power of the fox in order to keep it away. The *ararihua* becomes the fox, in other words, specifically in order to enforce one boundary – that between human and animal communities – and to cross over another – that between youth and adulthood.

The Andean fox's role as representative of that fluid, transitional space between two defined fields of existence is corroborated in an Inca story in which the fox is carried by the condor to a banquet in the sky. After eating, the fox tries to climb down a rope, but some parrots cut it so that he falls to earth and splatters his bones, hair, blood and the food he ate in all directions. On one level this story explains 'why there are now foxes everywhere', and, like other explanatory myths and fairy tales, this one says little about the fox, except that it is ubiquitous. But, as Urton justly points out, the myth also provides a primordial connection between foxes and agriculture. As transgressor of boundaries, the fox carries plants from heaven to earth, and then spreads 'cultivated plants between different ecological zones'.[19] In this sense, two familiar aspects stand out: the fox turns up everywhere, and he can easily cross the boundaries that restrict everyone else. The fox known to the Inca was the *culpeo*, which does not run away, but approaches closely to watch what people are doing. Understandably, this fox would figure more as a helper than a rogue; standing at the edge of family activity and unabashedly staring, the *culpeo* would seem to offer a guardianship, or a means of crossing the lines that divide society and wilderness, the different phases of life and the agricultural seasons or regions.

The fox is also called *Pascualito, hijo de la tierro*, or son of the earth, because he communicates with the earth and can hear through the earth about events far away, which also makes him *paqo*, or a diviner-curer.[20] This power of communication deriving from the fox's ubiquity, and from its close association with the earth, appears in almost every mythic system involving foxes, but, unlike Reynard, these Andean foxes primarily help human communities to understand the forces of nature and how to organize themselves along the model of nature.

William Morris,
*Colpeo Fox-head
Sculpture.*
William Morris
explores the
native mytho-
logy of the
Americas, re-
creating ancient
artefacts in glass
sculptures.

The fox's uncommon knowledge can thus provide a positive service to cultures that do not define themselves in opposition to nature, or that simply allow that different kinds of intelligence might function alongside each other. Among the Arctic peoples of North America and Siberia, the fox guides shamans through paths not ordinarily open or visible to humans, since it can burrow out of sight through brambles or the earth.[21] The fox's knowledge lies underground, beyond human understanding, and is identical with the living power of the earth, as the Quechua know who say that a fox seen travelling up or down a mountain, towards or away from the community, indicates where the harvest will succeed and where it will fail. The fox is both earthy and fleet, the flaming life that comes from the ground.

'Lindow Man', a 2,000 year-old British bog burial, with his fox-fur armband. The fiery red fox fur connected the human sacrifice with the primordial power of the earth that made crops grow.

The fiery significance of the fox is almost as ubiquitous and ancient as the animal itself, for evidence from archaeological sites in Britain and France indicate that vulpine fire was central to the Celts' ritual slayings.[22] The most famous slaying came to light as the Cheshire bog-body known as Lindow Man, who was strangled and buried in a marshy pool as part of a ritual sometime between the fourth century BC and the first century AD. That he was wearing nothing more than a boggy smile and a fox-fur armband suggests a vital connection between man and fox. Anne Ross asserts that the Celts used the fox's 'fiery red coat' in fire festivals seeking purification and protection for members of the community and their animals, and she describes the twentieth-century festival of Beltain in Perthshire honouring the god Belanos, in which people throw bread over their shoulder and say: 'I give this, oh fox, preserve my horses.'[23]

A more direct connection between the fox's fiery coat and literal flames appears in a description from first-century Rome by the poet Ovid. During the Cerialia – the festival of Ceres on 19 April – foxes with torches tied to their tails were made to run through the Circus Maximus until they burnt to death (*Fasti* IV. 681–712). This ritual immolation, according to Ovid, enacts the legend of a girl who wrapped a vixen in straw, then set it afire, letting it run into the cornfields and burn the crops. Ovid's legend recalls an equally brutal biblical scene describing how Samson, when having problems with the Philistines, angrily caught 300 foxes 'and he turned them tail to tail, and put a torch between each pair of tails. And when he had set fire to the torches, he let the foxes go into the standing grain of the Philistines, and burned up the shocks and the standing grain, as well as the olive orchards' (Judges 15: 4–6). The torches curiously make the fire redundant, since the fox's coat already provides the necessary image of fiery potency. What matters here is that the foxes should

Samson burning 300 foxes, in a wall painting from the Vatican Catacombs.

actually be given up in flames both to invoke and to seek redemption from the fox's power.

Among Druids, Sir James Frazer says, witches commonly disguised themselves as foxes, and burning alive was 'deemed the surest mode of getting rid of these noxious and dangerous beings'.[24] The immolation was not merely punishment, but the means of redirecting the fiery power into socially positive ends, for 'the Druids believed that the more persons they sentenced to death, the greater would be the fertility of the land'.[25] The habitation of the fox in the earth gives its fiery power a place among the most primordial chthonic forces of fertility. The ability of witches to disguise themselves as foxes reaffirms the fluid nature of vulpine power, which continually changes, just as cunning (or *metis*) does, shimmering, in Aesop's tale, like the leopard's varied coat.

The power of the vulpine shape-shifter has been explored more fully in Asia than anywhere else. In Japan the shape-shifting fox is the *kitsunē*, or spirit-fox, which has become an accepted figure in the Shinto religion. The Chinese spirit-fox is *Huli jing* (the fox itself is *hu*), or in older times, *Hujing*. The Chinese term *Laohu* refers to the Old Fox who has acquired, through his considerable age, the ability to change shape. Many of the tales and motifs familiar for centuries in oral versions were collected in the eighteenth century by prominent members of the elite society, like He Bang'e, who describes how he collected his stories during evenings when he and his friends would sit drinking: 'we extinguish candles and talk of ghosts, or converse on fox-spirits under the moonlight . . . To please myself I jot down all of these stories and over time have collected chapters full of them.'[26]

Commonly, the fox-spirits in these narratives take on the form of humans, and particularly beautiful young women, in order to involve themselves in the affairs of people who then

A Japanese print of a fox in moonlight.

have difficulty extricating themselves from the vulpine clutches. But foxes do not transform themselves only to have sex with humans or to amass wealth or knowledge, for they vary in their characters and motives just as much as people do, as becomes evident in the wide range of accounts of fox–human interactions. Fox-spirits are so plentiful that they and humans commonly become friends, cohabit the same house and even marry.

A spirit-fox disguising itself as a priest, from Tsukioka Yoshitoshi's series *100 Phases of the Moon*, 1886, woodblock print.

Because fox-spirits appear in so many roles – sometimes even employing their 'alchemical transformations' to seek enlightenment and to 'roam the islands of the immortals and ascend to celestial realms' – an uncertainty arises as to their real nature.[27] Ji Yun offers this explanation of where fox-spirits stand in relation to the other beings of the universe: 'Human beings and physical objects belong to two different categories; fox-spirits stand somewhere between the two. The paths of light and darkness never converge: fox-spirits stand somewhere between the two. Immortals and demons go different ways: fox-spirits stand somewhere between the two.'[28] Ji's explanation strikes a familiar chord in my survey of vulpine myths around the world. In natural histories as well as in myths and legend, the fox inhabits the margins between two opposed states – between forest and open field, or between social morality and unconventional intelligence. Like the fox that helps the young Inca man cross over into adulthood, Asian foxes belong to no single category of existence and so can pass from one to the other.

The spirit fox probably moved from China to Japan in the eighth century. The *Nihon Shoki* of AD 720 refers to the Japanese *kitsunē* as an animal of good omen, and in that same year the Emperor Gemmyo was presented with a black fox as a gift from Iga Province. By the ninth century, *kitsunē* had come to be associated with spirits through its identification with the god Inari, which might also – on one level – explain the attribution of shape-shifting powers, since Inari was originally a female deity associated with rice.[29]

In describing the female deity – who had been called *Uka no mitami no mikoto*, 'deity exalted spirit of food' – Kūkai (or Kōbō Daishi, AD 774–835) identified her with a different, masculine name, Inari. Thereafter Inari retained the association with food – rice in particular – and was known as the god who had changed both name and gender. By the Edo Period (1603–1867), Inari had come to be associated with his celestial foxes – two of which always guard his shrine, and one of which he rides – as much as with rice.[30] Shrines to Inari, including the pair of guardian foxes, spread with Buddhism throughout Japan,

Scroll of Inari riding the white fox.

Wooden Japanese Inari foxes.

Ceramic Japanese Inari foxes.

becoming so popular that a saying of the Edo Period was that 'Inari statues are as common as dog shit'.[31]

Already in the ninth century the ambiguous shape-shifting fox appeared in the collection *Nihon Ryōiki*, in stories of men marrying beautiful women who turn out to be foxes – for good or ill. In some stories, the couple have children who might themselves be foxes, or the fox is chased out of its human form to become some important landmark in the countryside, as in the famous tale of The Jewel Maiden from the twelfth century. This story looks to the court of the emperor Toba-no-in, where 'a mysterious woman of uncertain pedigree' becomes the emperor's favourite. She seldom leaves the emperor's side, and one night, when a storm blows out all the lamps, the mysterious woman radiates 'a light like the morning sun'. The emperor understands the event as proof of her spiritual cultivation, and names her Tamamo no mae, or the Jewel Maiden. When the emperor and his son grow ill, the court exorcist, Abe no Yasunari, performs a rite that expels Tamamo from the court, whereupon she turns back into a nine-tailed fox and flies off to the north-east – the direction from which demons influence human beings. Two warriors pursue her to Nasu moor in Shimotsuke province (modern Tochigi province), and, with the aid of the bodhisattva Kannon, kill the fox. Tamamo's spirit then assumes the form of a stone that emits poisonous airs, killing everything that comes near; this is known as the Murder Stone. A century later the Zen patriarch Gennō pacified the angry spirit and enshrined the stone in Nasuno as Sasahari Inari, where it remains today.[32]

The story of Tamamo no mai is probably the most retold of all the Japanese fox tales. Bathgate comments that versions appear 'in virtually every genre and medium from the fifteenth century until the nineteenth', and the Murder Stone became a famous travel destination, attracting the seventeenth-century poet Bashō.[33] This story epitomizes the spirit-fox as malevolent force, a version of the female vampire who destroys powerful men. What should also be noted is that in turning the fox to stone this story re-emphasizes the vulpine connection with the earth, bonding the fiery fluidity of its shape-shifting with its apparent opposite, foundational permanence.

Toba Sojo, drawing of a Japanese spirit-fox igniting its tail in order to assume human form, 12th century.

Often the Japanese stories focus on spirit foxes who use their shape-shifting powers to delude humans into believing that they are living in a mansion and dining on the finest of foods but are eventually found by their friends huddled in a burrow eating mice and twigs. This is the nutshell version of the Japanese story, 'The Fox-Wife of Bitchū', which developed out of the older Chinese stories of the fox as evil spirit sucking the life from the human victim. Leo Tak-hung Chan, commenting on the Chinese versions, explains that foxes acquire their shape-shifting power on the way towards spiritual enlightenment, but the ones who seduce humans are trying to shorten the process, and delude themselves as much as the humans.[34] These foxes represent an evil – or at least an immorality – that privileges pleasure, especially sexual pleasure, over spiritual advancement, and will not advance to higher life. It is their attempt to seduce humans that is dangerous.

The motif of the fox seducing humans has found a place in modern American and English fiction, as in Kij Johnson's syrupy retelling of 'The Fox-Wife of Bitchū 'in *Foxwoman* (2000), and (the much better) *Playing Foxes* (1988) by Helen Dixon, in which an English woman takes in an elusive Japanese lodger. But the most delightful by far is David Garnett's *Lady into Fox* (1923), which reverses the shape-shifting motif when Sylvia, wife of the long-suffering Mr Tebrick, decides to become a fox. These Westernized versions can only make fox lore into the exotic fantasies of romances and mysteries, however, because they wrest narratives and images from the living culture in which the tales have currency.

In Japan spirit-foxes are much more than the stuff of literature, for they really do take possession of people, and so commonly that fox-possession, or *kitsunē-tsuki*, has been considered for the past 900 years a dangerous disease. According to Nozaki, there are two types of *kitsunē-tsuki*. The first is possession by wild foxes (*nogitsunē*), a symptom of which is the victim shouting out something like 'I am the God of Inari, let me eat rice and beans'. In these cases the victim simply prays without consulting a physician. But in the second type, when a 'high-class' fox possesses a person, the victim will act like someone truly sick, and must be put under medical care.[35] The spirit-fox invades the body of a sufferer for a variety of reasons, such as simple malice, as revenge against the person who killed one of its young or woke it from an afternoon nap; or it may seek something unobtainable to one in fox form, such as fried tofu; or it may wish to have a shrine established to itself.

The cultural anthropologist Carmen Blacker relates how most of the exorcisms involve not the spirit-foxes that wilfully enter a person's body on their own, but those that are compelled to do so by ill-intentioned persons known as fox-employers, *kitsunē-tsukei*, or fox-owners, *kitsunē-mochi*, who get foxes with supernatural powers under their obligation by giving them food when they are hungry.[36] Families in rural Japan thought to be fox-owners are still ostracized for having amassed wealth unfairly by commanding their magical foxes to invade the bodies of other people. And, since all families need to resist the taint of fox-ownership, they will condemn any future bride who has even a distant relation thought to have owned foxes. The fear of fox-owners that pervades the countryside and all classes stands out in the following account from Blacker's personal experience:

> In the winter of 1963 I visited a temple called Taikyūji, not far from Tottori, which since the Meiji period had been a renowned centre for the exorcism of fox-possessed patients. The priest . . . had been the incumbent of the temple for twenty years and had exorcised a great many

fox-possessed people. It is easy to tell, he told me, who are the fox-owning families, because you can see the foxes sitting on the eaves of their roofs. Time and again during his evening stroll he had seen them playing outside the houses of the marked families, or sitting in a row on the eaves, shading their eyes with their paws. Often they would rush up to him, snarling and snapping at his robe. Nor was he the only one who could see them. Everyone in the village could do so.[37]

These ever-present spirit foxes require an acculturated vision to be recognized; thus Blacker the Westerner could not see the foxes that were plainly visible to everyone else. The fluid power of shape-shifting foxes has been recognized throughout the world, except in the West, which remains dominated by the Christian supression of alternate forces.

Japan is one of the modern societies in which an active fox lore continues. The features of this lore enforce the association of the fox with a shifting, elusive subterranean fire, as indicated by the rituals that foxes perform to become humans in which they pull their tail between their legs, and rub it with their forepaws until it ignites. It is not just the fiery red colour, but the flame-shaped tail that contains the power to change form. Over and again in stories throughout the world, the fox's tail is indicative of a fiery power. Among the Asian foxes, those who seek enlightenment for a thousand years acquire nine tails. In China the nine-tailed fox has its own name, *Jinwei hu*, while in Korea it is *Gumiho*, the fox that has become so powerful that it lives openly among humans (though it often gives itself away by being unable to hide its tail).

Bizarrely, this motif of nine tails turns up in the nineteenth-century Brothers Grimm story of 'Mrs Fox's Wedding', in which the old fox with nine tails feared that his wife is unfaithful. He plays dead, and suitors begin to appear seeking Mrs Fox's paw in marriage. The first fox to come a-courting has only one tail, the second two, and so on, until one appears with nine tails, just as her husband had. When Mrs Fox is about to marry this new-comer with nine tails, the original Mr Fox rises up and chases everyone, including Mrs Fox, from the house. The first fox that comes to woo with only one tail is identified in this story as 'young' and Mr Fox himself is described as 'old', but beyond that there is nothing in this European account that explicitly con-nects the addition of tails to power.

Ruth Battigheimer would disagree, however, since she iden-tifies the nine tails as a double entendre underscoring the sexual inadequacy of Mrs Fox's first eight suitors: 'For in German, tail (*Schwanz*) also means *cock* or *prick*', an interpretation corrob-orated by the illustration of the *kitsunē* rubbing his tail through his legs.[38] And, furthermore, Volker points out that animals with multiplied body parts serve as a common motif on the decor-ated Japanese *netsukē* – the toggle used to lock the cord of the pouch in which a person kept his or her possessions, and that the high number of fox images used in the *netsukē* is due to its role as symbol for a February day dedicated to celebrating the phallus fertility cult.[39]

But what remains unanswered is how two nineteenth-century German collectors of folk tales should have encountered a motif that was already bizarre when it passed from China to Japan and Korea in the ninth century. In the early 1980s the literary scholar John M. Ellis presented his controversial argument that the Grimms were not wholly truthful in presenting their *Märchen* as the oral tales of common German folk, but that they had derived most of the stories from bourgeois friends, who got them from foreign books.[40] So the possibility of an Asian

Japanese Kabuki
fox mask.

source for 'The Marriage of Mrs Fox' certainly exists, even though the Grimms retained only the phallic association without the venerable enlightenment.

Whether the vulpine tail signifies a higher understanding or simply another phallus, the common thread running through the different mythic systems is that the fox embodies a primordial force that mainstream doctrine tries to conceal. The ambiguity of the power that can appear positive in a culture like the Inca and negative in western Europe is what Asian myths explore so richly. But most notable is the fact that so many different cultures have developed myths and legends around this one animal, illustrating the persistence of an ancient subterranean vulpine fire that insinuates itself into daily life and language.

3 The Linguistic Fox

The word *fox* can refer to a wide range of behaviours, appearances and, as the previous chapter showed, religious and legendary meanings and associations. This is true not only in European languages, but in Japan as well, where the spirit-fox possesses several names besides *kitsunē*, such as *ninko*, the man-fox, *yako*, the field-fox, and *kuda*, the pipe fox.[1] All these names reflect regional variations on the central figure of the spirit-fox and indicate the varied associations that the spirit-fox may have among the people of different localities.[2] These associations affect the way that people understand other objects in the world – such as the plants that spirit-foxes might use – and illustrate how flexible the connotations of the word 'fox' might be in daily speech. And since these colloquial metaphorical meanings often carry more force than the literal dictionary sense of the word, they can often tell us a great deal about people's attitudes towards the object literally designated by the word. All the different ways in which the word 'fox' can be used reflect not only the qualities of the animal in nature but its roles in myths and folk tales, and very often have little or nothing to do with the animal itself.

In Japan the fear of being led astray by an untrustworthy spirit-fox is so pervasive that a set of social conventions has arisen by which people can assure one another of their humanness. In telephone conversations such assurances are especially important, since the two parties cannot see each other and have to rely entirely on verbal codes. One convention has it that foxes cannot pronounce certain sounds in human speech, such as the phrase *moshi moshi*, which has become the standard telephone greeting and has no real meaning beyond demonstrating that the speaker can make non-vulpine sounds. In effect, then, the greeting means 'rest assured that you are not speaking to a spirit-fox who might trick you'.[3]

Notably, then, because Japan and Christian Europe have the most developed traditions around the fox, these two cultures have made most use of it to codify other animals, objects and actions. Both these cultures also appear to have used the fox linguistically in much the same way, as a reference to certain characteristics to be recognized in something that is not itself a fox. Asian and European speakers both have the red fox in mind, simply because this is the species that has become so widespread as to be declared 'common'. When the fox referent is applied to other animals it is supposedly because those animals hold some physical resemblance to the red fox, mostly in the face. The exceptions to be noted at the outset are the British dogs – foxhounds and fox terriers – whose names refer not to their appearance but to the historical reason they were created as breeds. But overall the reference to foxy looks is actually more complicated than it seems at first, simply by the number of animals described as 'foxy'.

Dogs are often described as being 'foxy' when their face is triangular, their ears pricked and their muzzle long, narrow and pointed, as with the schipperke. Likewise in Japan, *Kitsunē-zaru*, or fox monkey, is the name of a long-nosed, pointed-eared lemur. Three different fishes, the *Kitsunē-tai*, *Kitsunē-tara* and *Kitsunē-koi* – or fox-sea bream, fox-cod and

A Delmarva fox squirrel.

The fox sparrow, a North American bird somewhat larger than European sparrows. Note the fox-coloured feathers.

Flying Fox by Vincent van Gogh, 1886, oil on canvas.

fox-carp, respectively – all have vulpine noses, and at least one is red. The facial quality of the fox appears as the distinguishing feature of some other animals as well, such as the North American fox squirrel, so-called because of its long ears. The flying fox (*megachiroptera*) is a bat found in Africa, southern Asia and Australia whose large pointed ears and nose call to mind those of Reynard. The fact that these animals are designated not at all by what they are – dog, lemur, fish, squirrel, bat – but by their superficial resemblance to a fox, to which they otherwise hold no meaningful relation whatsoever, alerts us to the metaphorical power of the fox in both Asian and European cultures. Because fox characters figure so largely in the literature of Asia and Europe, the animal itself holds a wide-ranging referential power that might go no further than identifying physical qualities, like the long nose of the schipperke or the pointed ears of the fox squirrel, but could also identify a non-physical quality, as with the flying fox, which has the expected facial features of pointy nose and ears, but also the distinction of being hated as an invasive and dirty pest (which probably explains why it is not just a 'fox-bat' – a name that would signify that the animal is a bat with foxy looks – but a fox that flies, and thereby indicating just how much it is hated). Nor does the

A North
American
fox snake.

fox snake (*Elaphe vulpina*), common in the American states
along the northern Mississippi River, have anything like a foxy
face, or even an orange colour; rather, it earns its name through
a musky smell reminiscent of the fox's.

Associations with foxes are often not even based on similarities, but derive from the indirect associations formed with fox
characters in folklore. Because the Japanese spirit-foxes developed a culture parallel to that of humans, a number of plants
are identified by their supposed use among *Kitsunē*. *Kitsunē-
azami*, a type of aster, is the 'fox's powder-brush'. *kitsunē-no-
karakasa*, which belongs to the saxifrage family, provides 'fox's
umbrella'. *Kitsunē-no-kanzashi*, a black alder, serves as the 'fox's
ornamental hairpin'. *Kitsunē-no-makura*, a gourd, is the 'fox's
pillow'. *Kitsunē-no-kamisori*, a poisonous member of *Lycoris
radiata*, provides the 'fox's razor'; the mushroom, *Kitsunē-no-
rosoku*, the 'fox's candle'; and *kitsunē-no-wan*, another fungus,
serves as the 'fox's wooden bowl'. Since a dominant motif of the
kitsunē stories involves the discovery that what the deluded person had thought were luxurious furnishings and food turn out
to be sticks and leaves, the attribution of so many plants to
vulpine usage is not so surprising.[4]

The Fox's Penis mushroom, from an early print. This fungus earns its name from the strong sexual associations of the *kitsunē*.

The 'fox's penis', or *kitsunē-no-chimpo*, makes a somewhat different suggestion about the role of the *kitsunē* myths generally. A tall mushroom that does, in fact, resemble an erect penis, *Kitsunē-no-chimpo* alerts us to the aura of sexuality pervading the *kitsunē* stories, for a good number of the tales revolve around the theme of people being deluded by foxes who want them for sex. And this is not the last connection we shall find between foxes and sex; but it is significant, since the mushroom, like the fox, is so closely associated with the earth, denoting a sexuality that is irresistible – and socially illegitimate – because it is chthonic.

Plants in Britain and America notable for their identification with (or as) foxes include the fox-grape, so called because its flavour is suitable only for unrefined palates, and again calling to mind the rankness of the fox. But without doubt, the best-known vegetative vulpine is the foxglove. This plant carries a long history of fox lore, for it has also been called 'fox-bells', from the time when the belief that fox-tails would ward off the Devil ensured that foxes were vigorously hunted for their brushes: fearing extinction, the foxes turned for help to their vulpine gods who put bells throughout the fields to warn them of the hunters. When the fox-tails lost their potency against the Devil and foxes were no longer threatened by superstitious hunters, the bells also lost their sound. The foxglove turns up in Anglo-Saxon as *foxes glōfa*, since the flowers resemble the fingers of gloves; correspondingly, the Irish name for the flower is *méríní puca* – fairy fingers – while in Wales they are goblins' gloves, and in Yorkshire witches' thimbles. A popular etymology thus has 'foxglove' originating from 'folk's glove', once worn by the little people, or folk, who in turn showed their friends, the foxes, how to use the flowers as gloves to muffle their footfalls while sneaking into the chicken coops at night.

76

The foxglove, in a 19th-century handbook. The flowers of *Digitalis purpurea* were given to foxes by fairies to soften their footfalls as they sneaked into henhouses.

This same identification with fingers suggested itself to the German botanist Leonhard Fuchs – whose name coincidentally means 'fox' – and who gave the flower its scientific name of *Digitalis*, which is the Latin for 'of the finger', since the common German name for it is *Fingerhut*, or thimble. Even in the dry nomenclature of science, we find a foxy wit tunnelling through the narrative of this flower's history, for Fuchs was honoured by Linnaeus, who gave his name to the *Fuchsia*. These bright red flowers have not only lent their vulpine label to the colour we associate with them, but to the aniline dye, fuchsin, used in inks and colouring agents to achieve that colour (chemically, $C_{20}H_{19}N_3HCl$). And as long as we are on the topic of German foxes, or *Fuchsen*, it is worth noting that another Fuchs, this one the mineralogist Johann Nepomuk von Fuchs, gave his name to the mica now commonly called 'fuchsite'. Animal, vegetable and mineral, the fox dons many disguises, and has become a common surname for many people.

Families named Fox, or Todd (Scottish for fox), along with Fuchs, Reynard (or Renard) and the Dutch Voss, all hold direct identification with the fox, which raises the question of why families would adopt that characterization in the first place. The Fox clan in Ireland has traced the history of their name, which can appear as Fox or as the Irish Sionnach or Shionnaighe, or the anglicized Irish of Shinnick. Although the clan has ties to fourth-century patriarchs, the actual use of the name Fox first appears in the eleventh century, when Tadhg O'Catharnaigh – whose first name means Fox – repeatedly out-witted his martial opponents through tactics they considered unfair. An alternate history suggests that the family became associated with the fox when they killed the poet Cuan Ua Lothchain and were thereafter marked with a noxious fox-like smell – although what mystical power chose to avenge the poet in this particular fashion remains unclear.[5]

In the case of the American Indian tribe of Foxes, any mean-ingful explanation must be speculative, since they have few if any records, prior to the European invasion, of the origin of their iden-tification. The Algonquin name *Wakoha* means 'a person of the Fox clan'; and *wakošeha* refers to the animal itself.[6] But the reason why the *Wakoha* identified themselves with the *wakošeha* cannot be determined, except as an indication of clan relation that repli-cates the observed division of animal species, since within the larger tribal families, or gens, groups named themselves after ani-mals and natural forces. So a person may be *Wakoha* and belong to the Sturgeon gens or the Thunder gens within the tribe. Such layered identifications of people with animals reflect the complex relations among human and animal families in the Andean

Quechua, and give strong credence to the notion that they originated in much the same way as the European clan names, as epithets carrying multiple cultural associations.

The Sac tribe – allied with the Foxes in the early 1700s – produced a leader in the nineteenth-century struggle to retain traditional territories whose name was *Keokuk*, or the Watchful Fox (1790–1840), even though he was a Sac and not *Wakoha*. His name identified neither his tribal nor his family affiliation, but rather his own personal character, which manifested itself through complicated negotiations with representatives of the United States government. The Watchful Fox is memorialized by the town of Keokuk, Iowa, near the area where the Sac and Fox people sojourned from 1833 to 1846, as the US government forcibly moved the tribes further and further from ancestral

Keokuk, chief of the Sacs & Foxes, hand-coloured litho-graph, 1838.

lands. After 1846 the two tribes were transferred to Kansas, where they stayed for 23 years before being made to move to the Oklahoma territory – long the refuge of people banned from every other place. Except for a contingent of Foxes who returned to Iowa in 1851, the Sac and Fox Nation retains its granted land in Oklahoma to this day.

Chances are that the identification of European clans with the fox began as an epithet assigned to (or hurled at) the family or individual whom their opponents looked upon with all the anger that comes from losing to someone who has not fought fairly. This supposition gains affirmation from three modern-day military foxes. When Napoleon referred to General Mikhail Kutuzov as 'the fox of the North', the Corsican was not praising his Russian counterpart but rather deriding him for refusing to stay put long enough to be beaten properly. The same frustration motivated the British Lieutenant-Colonel Banastre Tarleton, who gave up

The Swamp Fox, a 19th-century depiction of Lieut.-Colonel Francis Marion in the swamps of South Carolina.

his chase of the American Francis Marion through the swamps of South Carolina with the comment 'as for this damned old fox, the Devil himself could not catch him'. The epithet acquired its positive quality when the story of Tarleton's fear of entering the swamps spread among the local inhabitants, who then raised Marion as a folk hero, eluding English law through native wit.[7]

Probably the most famous military fox of the twentieth century was Erwin Rommel, the Desert Fox, who frustrated the Allies on several occasions during the North Africa campaign of the Second World War. As with the Russian and American martial foxes, the German Rommel became something of a legendary character, even among his enemies, by repeatedly eluding capture and assassination. The magical power of the Desert Fox became so famous that Field-Marshal Sir Claude Auchinleck issued an order stating: 'There exists a real danger that our friend Rommel is becoming a kind of magician or bogey-man to our troops, who are talking far too much about him.'[8] The fear of the magical Desert Fox was interwoven with the usual denigration of vulpines, that he lacked strategy vital to the proper waging of war, and that his skill lay only in fox-like tactics that enabled him to deceive and elude his pursuers.

Rommel (left), the famous 'Desert Fox', among his Afrika Korps veterans.

The name of Fox among Celtic tribes could also, then, hold this suggestion of a magical, primordial power. In speculating on why the Lindow Man should wear a fox-fur armlet, Miranda Green comments that the 'name Louernius means "son of the Fox", and belonged to an Avernian chief: Athenaeus comments on his immense wealth and his practice of holding great festive gatherings in a huge enclosure at which he liberally distributed largesse in the form of treasure to his people'.[9] Green offers no more suggestion about what the 'ritual association with foxes' might entail; but the wealth and generosity of Louernius, Son of the Fox, would indicate that he possessed a certain kind of power, manifested in the beneficence he bestowed in festive displays.

A large concern of my discussion of fox names – and of foxes generally – is directed towards the idea that cultures around the world have given this animal a peculiar standing among other creatures by investing it with a power fluid and indeterminate enough to hold variable and even contradictory values. This vulpine force has long been associated with fire, as indicated by the story of Samson, but 'foxfire', as a term in its own right, carries a range of possible references. Direct associations between fire and the fox are easily created by the animal's colour (at least that of *V. vulpes*), its physical litheness and the glow of its eyes in the dark. Its burrowing habits, along with its talents for disguise and evasion, qualify that association into a fire that works secretly, and perhaps with a certain degree of exclusivity. The person who possessed that foxfire would be named accordingly, and Louernius's filial relation to the fox would also suggest that, as with the Quechua whose uncle is the fox, he is guided by the animal and is himself vulpine through actual inheritance. The lineal descent of foxfire would seem to occur in much the same way as royal appointment. Those who possess the strange and elusive power not only have it, but *are* it; everyone else may simply admire or fear it, but, try as we will, unless we inherit the foxfire we can never obtain it.

In Japan foxfire – or *kitsunē-bi* – is described as a sport among the *kitsunē*. The fox that desires to take on human form rubs its tail until it ignites. The suggestion is that the fox stimulates the fire of life itself in order to alter its form, as though it were an alchemist. Nozaki lists four other versions of foxfire: when a host of small lights shine in the distance; when a few fire balls pass by; when the windows of several large buildings are all illuminated; and when the processional of *kitsunē-no-yomēiri* – the fox wedding – lights its way through the forest, indicated by the sun shining through the falling rain.[10] These different types of *kitsunē-bi* all share the common quality of elusiveness; they might be startling, as with the fire balls, or even spectacular, as with the illuminated windows, but they all resist containment and domestication by the human world: we cannot bring any version of *kitsunē-bi* or foxfire home to warm our tea kettle. The mysterious illuminations remind us that both to the Asian and the Western mind, foxes, and the strange powers they represent, lie in wait just outside the safety of our homes and cities ready to trick us – or even to take possession of us.

Because the associations we attach to words change constantly, what one generation might take for granted as an implied meaning of a word may be lost entirely on another. It is in these implicit connotations of a word that much of its cultural currency actually exists, however, and so to learn what a word fully meant at a given moment requires that some of those connotations be recovered. At some point, and it would seem to be in the second half of the twentieth century, the American and European fox came to hold a complex of sexual meanings. In their old *Saturday Night Live* routine of The Wild and Crazy Guys, Steve Martin and Dan Akroyd were always out to get some foxes. Jimi

Uma Thurman in *Pulp Fiction*. Her character stars in a show called *Fox Force Five*.

Hendrix, never known for the subtlety of his lyrics, sang of 'a cute little heart breaker', his foxy lady. Exactly which vulpine quality signifies the lady's sexual appeal remains unstated, and unstatable. In the film *Pulp Fiction*, when Mia Wallace, played by Uma Thurman, describes to John Travolta the pilot film she made, she says the title was 'Fox Force Five', fox because the main characters are all foxy chicks, force because they are a force to be reckoned with, and five because there are one, two, three, four, five of them. (The title also alludes to *Foxforce*, the blaxsploitation and martial arts film of 1976 by Cirio H. Santiago, which bears the alternate titles *Ebony, Ivory and Jade* and *She Devils in Chains*.) Understanding perfectly that the five women in the pilot were to be presented more as sex objects than as defenders of civil liberties, we can assume a parallel between the vulpine physique and that of Uma Thurman and her four forceful colleagues (similar to Chaucer's description of Alison in 'The Miller's Tale' as having a body like a weasel). But much of the sexual value of the term obviously originates from the hunt, where the fox serves as the prey to the sexual adventurer, which in this case would make the sexual epithet applicable to either gender. And I would be remiss if I

Fox Fires on New Year's Eve at the Enoki Tree, by Ando Hiroshige, 1857, woodblock print.

85

overlooked the phonic quality of the word 'fox' in the sexual context, which makes it very close to the slang term, either noun or verb, for the sex act. Some astute film critics have said that Thurman intentionally mumbles the title of her character's pilot to reinforce its sexual aspect subliminally (a point made less subtly in the film *Used Cars*, in the repeated references to a character named Fuchs who has screwed everyone else).

Outside the sexual arena, the animal may become a verb, 'to fox', which predictably can refer to several, very different, actions. In the world of printmaking, 'to fox' a sheet of paper is to stain it – and in fact this sense has come to refer to staining generally. Cobblers, before footwear became mass-produced disposable items, would 'fox' a boot or shoe by renewing the upper leather, though the term can also refer to the addition of leather for purely decorative purposes. Thus, a man who had had his boots newly 'foxed' might choose to show them off by wearing them as he rode his hot-blooded horse where everyone could admire his taste and wealth. Naturally, he would want to display his horsemanship as well as his wardrobe, and so would require his groom 'to fox' his mount's ears, and they would be dutifully trimmed.

Where these vulpine verbs originate I do not know. But I can say that after a good ride – or after any other activity, for that matter – nothing tastes better than a pint of beer. If the beer has gone sour, however, I would say to the landlord that it has 'foxed', or is 'foxy'. The supposed reason here is that foxy beer deranges the stomach to act as an emetic, and at the same time it cunningly disrupts the drinker's rational thoughts.

The fox might be said to govern almost all aspects of the sport of drinking. Samuel Pepys wrote of his evening out on 23 April 1661: 'I drank so much I was almost foxed.' The *Oxford English Dictionary* provides a slightly earlier, and active, usage of the transitive verb from Tarlton's *Jests* of 1621: 'Before they parted they *foxt* Tarlton at the Castle in Pater Noster Row.' John Minsheu, an early lexicographer and an exceedingly temperate man into the bargain, wrote in 1599 that 'Whosoever loves a good wine, hunts the fox once a year.' Pepys seems to have experienced a few more hangovers than Minsheu, and would have complained of 'flaying the fox', a phrase said to originate as a literal translation of the French *écorcher le renard*, used by Rabelais to describe Gargantua's frequent habit of throwing up after drinking.[11] The French still use a variant of the phrase, saying *piquer un renard*, or 'to prick a fox', as suffering from a hangover, and in the church of St Fiacre, near Le Faouët in Brittany, a woodcarving depicts a man holding a wine cask on his left knee and with a half-flayed fox hanging out of his mouth. The position of the fox running down the man's chest and stomach represents the wine-dark vomit covering the tunic of a drunkard like Gargantua, depicting the reference to staining as well as to the more direct reference to Gargantua's feelings on the morning after having chased the fox.

Just as the game of love makes use of the fox to describe all aspects of sexual activity, so drinking employs it to identify the three fundamental stages of bibulism. The drinker hunts the fox, gets – or is – foxed, and then flays the fox as he finds his shirt foxed. But whereas sexual fox references allude to the association

The fox carving in St Fiacre, Le Faouët. Having chased the fox, the drunken monk flays the fox.

between foxes and fire, bibulous fox phrases do not seem to go beyond the word itself. The attraction that the word 'fox' holds for drinking terms can be understood, however, in looking back to the sexual use. When Uma Thurman mumbles 'Fox Force Five', she plays on the phonic similarity between 'fox' and the slang word for coitus, the 'f-word', so dreaded in America, and which seventeenth- and eighteenth-century English writers cast as 'f—k', as in the Earl of Rochester's 'Much wine had passed, with grave discourse / Of who f—ks who and who does worse' ('A Ramble in St James's Park', 1–2). The nearly homonymous relation between 'fox' and 'f—ks' allows the delicate drinker to refer to the stages of his sport without offending either the landlord or other patrons in the hostelry. So, to say, 'Sir, I am nearly foxed' holds much the same phonic value – and therefore the same meaning – as the somewhat less understated expression, 'Dude, I'm really f—ked'.

The final predicative use of the fox is associated with the English sword named for the fox – albeit mistakenly, since the name refers to what is actually a small wolf on the blade. So 'to fox' someone is to stab them with the fox (sword). What is interesting about this otherwise innocuous definition is that it accords with the allegorical view from the Middle Ages that the fox injures the earth by burrowing in it, just as Satan digs into the hearts of the people he corrupts. The Japanese also have a small sword, *ko kitsunē-maru*, which was made at the command of Emperor Ichijō (987–1011) by the renowned swordsmith Munechika. As recounted in the Kabuki play by Sanjyo Kokaji, the god Inari sent one of his white fox messengers to help Munechika; the fox wielded the smith's younger hammer during the forging, and so the sword won the name *ko kitsunē-maru*, which means Young Fox, or Little Fox.[12]

As if the range of vulpine references were not broad enough, the fox's tail introduces an entirely new set of possibilities. As we

Foxtail grass, found throughout northern temperate regions.

shall see, value accrues to the fox's tail when it becomes one of the trophies of fox-hunting. But Aesop also emphasizes the importance of the tail in identifying the fox, as in 'The Fox without a Tail', where a fox loses his tail in a trap and becomes 'so much ashamed of his appearance that he thought life was not worth living'.[13] The fox's embarrassment shows how closely the human imagination identifies the tail with the fox, so that the tail serves as the most common symbol for the whole animal along with its cultural and verbal associations. Because of its shape, and because of the notable white tip accentuating the red-orange fur, the tail reinforces once again the vulpine connection with fire. The shape in a more neutral sense would explain the association with fox-tail grass, *Alopecurus pratensis*. And, combined with the burrowing habits of the fox, the tail's dimensions would also account for the connection with the wedge – known as the fox-tail – driven into a bolt to tighten it within the fastening nut.

The shape does not explain the fox-tail's more notable signifying function – long before the advent of fox-hunting – as the mark of the fool. Rabelais says that any man whose coat of arms indulges in puns to signify with an object what he cannot identify with a word 'ought to have a fox's tail tied to his collar and his nose rubbed in a cowpat'.[14] Why the fox-tail should come to signify the fool is unclear, but William Empson makes a few suggestions. 'A major activity of the Fool', he says, was 'to make a fool of other people'. And the activities of the fool, which often included revenge upon those who had injured him, created the view among his victims that 'the fool got more pleasure out of life than the virtuous, so was positively more sensible'.[15] If the fox-tailed fool is condemned for having more fun than the rest of us, then his connection with the folklore of Reynard is obvious, especially given a statement like the one from Samuel Purchas's *Pilgrimage* quoted in the *Oxford English Dictionary*: 'Such a one is carried about the towne with a boord fastned to his necke, all behanged with foxe-tayles.' The procession of the fool here holds a strong connection to the procession of all the animals carrying Reynard to the gallows, when the fox has been condemned precisely for enjoying himself at others' expense. The fox-tail, as Empson makes clear, would not be the badge of imbecility but of the wily character who dupes the virtuous.

Linguistic references to the fox, like the fox itself, are almost ubiquitous and adaptable to widely different contexts. 'Fox' can mean colour, fire, sexiness, smell, intelligence, immorality; it can refer to a host of non-vulpine objects, animals, plants, minerals and actions; it can identify clans in Europe and America, and relations within clans. In Europe and Asia the linguistic usage of 'fox' reflects the literary traditions that impute ethical lapses to the animal that are then associated with undesirable human behaviour. The associations assigned by these traditions to the fox can sometimes be tied to actual observable vulpine behaviours, but very often they are wholly literary. After the nineteenth century, the fox acquired an entirely new set of cultural associations, however, which we shall next examine in the artistic and literary depictions of fox-hunting.

4 Fox-hunting

Just as the linguistic appearances of the fox reflect the mythic heritage of the animal, so the ways in which people interact with the fox itself – through hunting and commerce – reflect the increasingly secular view of nature that Western society has developed since the seventeenth century. Mythic tales of foxes account for primordial forces that may both hinder and help humans, but by the 1600s depictions in literature and painting of the fox being hunted no longer evoked the fiery power of the primordial earth; instead, the fox was vermin – a pest that needed to be destroyed. This change was an almost exclusively Western event, since the Aristotelian view that only humans were capable of rational deliberation grew into the Christian tradition that saw animals as soulless, mindless bodies with which human beings – with their intellect and language – had little in common. As Keith Thomas argues, this division between humans and animals provides a partial explanation for the fact that Europeans of the sixteenth and seventeenth centuries 'were exceptionally carnivorous by comparison with the vegetable-eating peoples of the East'.[1]

Fox-hunting has been uneasily connected to the Western habits of meat eating that have justified hunting, since the odorous red fox is not generally considered edible. The reactionary writer Roger Scruton – who took up the cause of fox-hunting late in life – sneers at those 'fastidious aesthetes' who find fox flesh noxious. As a counter to daintiness, Scruton provides his own well-tried recipe for vulpine stew, which, as coincidence would have it, is almost the exact one followed by Werner Herzog in Les Blank's film *Werner Herzog Eats his Shoe* (1980).[2]

Scruton's silly attempt to transform fox-hunting into a utilitarian act of food-gathering makes the hollowness of all such justifications painfully obvious. The persistence of fox-hunting depends wholly on the low regard in which the fox is held in Western culture. As animal rights organizations arose during the nineteenth century, considerable attention was given to the treatment of horses and hounds while the fox was disregarded as vermin, and unworthy of protection.[3] This division among animals that makes some species better than others is an extension of the way that fox-hunting has reflected class divisions in Britain; attempts to justify it as part of the natural harmony of the countryside call up the larger argument that a natural basis exists for class or racial divisions in human society.

Thus it is that the history of fox-hunting in England reflects deep changes in English culture, including the agricultural revolutions that physically reshaped the countryside and created wholly new breeds of horses and hounds, and the economic shift from the eighteenth-century land-based society of inherited privilege to the more mobile bourgeois society driven by new capital. The year 1753 is generally recognized as the start of the great age of English fox-hunting, because this was when one of its most influential proponents, Hugo Meynell, took over as master of the most prominent hunt, the Quorn. And 1914, the start of the First World War, is the date usually given as the end of that great age, because fox-hunting never again held the prominence to which it had risen by the mid-nineteenth century. That fox-hunting should now be surrounded by controversy,

George Morland's *Fox Hunting: The Death*, 1801, oil on canvas.

that it should give rise to such strong feelings for and against, can perhaps be taken as a symptom of yet another turn in the cultural history of Britain (and elsewhere, for fox-hunting is no less controversial in North America, and is opposed and defended with virtually the same rhetoric as in Britain). My desire is not to enter the fray on either side, but only to describe what has happened to the fox itself during this great age when depictions of actual hunts reflect the changes in society and the landscape as well as in the attitudes towards animals.

Here it is important to note that just as foxes were hunted in England well before 1753, so they have also long been hunted outside the British Isles. In Virginia, George Washington established his own pack of hounds in 1767 and was already hunting foxes for sport several years before that. Hunts proliferated throughout America, although the grey fox's woodland habits never allowed for the long, fast rides characteristic of the English hunt. As the range of red foxes spread throughout the United

States, however, the hunts emulated the English mode more closely – and continue to do so. Australians began importing foxes in 1845 to supply the gap in their social life, though they seem to have neglected to catch their prey, for by 1893 a fox bounty was established in a futile effort to prevent the introduced predator from destroying the native fauna. But it was in late eighteenth-century England that fox-hunting developed into the sport that people customarily envision when they hear or read about specifically bred hounds chasing a fox over the picture-postcard landscape of open fields and hedgerows, while well-dressed people ride behind on thoroughbreds.

Depictions of fox-hunting before 1753 coincide with the characterizations of Reynard as an outlaw, and the view of foxes more broadly as nuisances that of necessity had to be purged but that provided little merit to the hunter who killed them. The status of the fox has not changed; what has is the value of fox-hunting as a sport, due to specific historical events starting with the extinction of stags, the traditional prey of the royal hunt. By the middle of the seventeenth century the deer had been almost entirely exterminated in England, and, during the Civil War, Parliament ordered the wholesale slaughter of deer in the royal parks as a way of cutting out the royal hold over the land. Killing the royal deer struck a blow at the Game Laws, which royalty and nobles had used for centuries to maintain their privilege and power over other classes by determining who had the right to enter forests and kill game. So, by the time of the Restoration in 1660, just as the legal right to hunt was extended to other classes, the stags had become simply too scarce to hunt.

Foxes had long been hunted, and in fact bounties had been placed on them to encourage their destruction. As hunting rights spread, and the other animals traditionally hunted from horses disappeared, sportsmen looked to foxes, who gave good

Within the image: `. FOX HVNTING .`

With Eger Hounds, the Fox is hard purfu'd · | Theire noble chafe, and fhew'd them Princely Sport
Till him they Earth, whofe Subtile fhifts renew'd | Whofe Death the Cuntrey pleafes as the Court :

Fox Hunting, an
engraving by
Wenceslas Hollar
(1607–77) after
a design by
Francis Barlow
(c. 1626–1704).

chase and whose destruction could be called a 'community
service'.[4] Depictions of fox-hunting reflected the changes in
the English landscape and in class structure, but it was only
very late in the history of the sport that they showed any change
in how the fox was thought of.

The seventeenth-century artist Francis Barlow depicted
foxes being hunted by hounds in scenes that preserve the differences from the modern hunt as it developed a century later.
In the picture illustrated here the hunt takes place in a woodland, and over unsteady terrain. The hounds are heavy Talbots,
slow movers who patiently follow a scent, suited to the woodlands that existed before the eighteenth-century enclosures.
The huntsman following the hounds is afoot, and carries a pole
to aid in digging up the fox, which is just about to go to earth.
This scene depicts a fox-hunt that would be very close to that
enjoyed by the Comte de Buffon in eighteenth-century France –
and, with its combination of qualified hunters riding and

unqualified hunt servants on foot, it indicates how hunting has always retained its royal associations, since hunting from horses was imagined to replicate the royal hunts that prepared the king and his nobles for war.

As sportsmen turned out of necessity from stags to foxes, sport painters sought to retain the drama of the traditional kill scene. The tragedy of the majestic, antlered stag inevitably succumbing to the numerous hounds was transformed into the fox as the emblem of violent, untamed nature, out-fought in close combat by trained and well-bred hounds. English sport painters took their cue in depicting the drama of hunting from various French masters, among them Jean-Baptiste Oudry (1686–1755), whose hunt scenes were popular enough to be reproduced as tapestries and as decorations on furniture and weapons. *The Death of the Fox* is typical of Oudry's emphasis on 'the grand ceremonial of the kill that provided the moment of truth for those few eligible by birth and position to participate' in the hunt.[5] The savagery of this depiction is in accord with Oudry's other paintings of hounds killing stags and boars. The fox here is not running away from the hounds but is boldly confronting its opponents; in fact, the fox, with its bared teeth, its aggressive stance and its muscular body, appears far more savage and less sympathetic than the hounds, whose teeth are mostly concealed and whose faces express desperation and fear. These hounds could be our pets, while Reynard embodies the untamed violence of nature. It is not the low thief that we see in this picture, but the awful predator feared by the Thebans, who marked the beginning of their cultural history with the liberation from such a beast.

The savagery of Oudry's painting appealed to the British painters Thomas Gainsborough and Sawrey Gilpin. By the time these two artists presented their versions of a kill, fox-hunting had already developed in England beyond anything comparable

The Death of the Fox, Jean-Baptiste Oudry, 1725, oil on canvas.

on the Continent. Although kill scenes by Gainsborough and Gilpin significantly differ from Oudry's in casting the fox as the victim, they still emphasize the violence of the hunt, which later artists subdued.

In Gainsborough's *Greyhounds Coursing a Fox* (1785), the fox has become the victim: even the gesture of baring its teeth seems pitiful in light of its impending violent death. Tension comes not from a conflict of equal opponents, but from the visual anguish of the fox run down by dispassionate killers whose size and number it cannot match. Notably absent from Gainsborough's depiction of coursing are the people who set

Thomas Gainsborough, *Greyhounds Coursing a Fox* (1785), oil on canvas.

their dogs on foxes for the sport of seeing which dog could run down and kill the victim fastest. Following Oudry, Gainsborough highlighted the visual qualities of animal violence, and chose to avoid the moral comment that the depiction of any human reaction would have suggested, but in excluding the people from his painting, he overlooks the 'sporting' element to depict only the violence.

Sawrey Gilpin's *Death of the Fox* (1793) was made eight years after Gainsborough's *Coursing*, but still early enough for the violence to be plain and straightforward. The fox in the painting has clearly reached the end of its run, and the foxhounds definitely have their blood up, as they swarm in from almost every direction. The hounds' faces, with teeth bared and eyes bulging, bespeak the frenzy of pack mentality, as individual hounds clamber over each other for a taste of 'Charlie's' blood.[6] Unlike Gainsborough, Gilpin includes the human members of the hunt, but only as ancillary actors, obscuring them either by shadow or distance.

The violence of the scenes by Gainsborough and Gilpin reflects the way that the members of the hunt field saw themselves – and were seen by others – during this time. Gilpin executed his *Death of the Fox* at the behest of his patron, Colonel Thomas Thornton, who wanted to commemorate the successful end to a 23-mile run. Gilpin originally painted a life-sized version of the scene, using as his models some of Thornton's hounds, which were themselves killed so that they might be posed in suitable positions. The large original has been lost, but, fortunately, the painting proved so popular that Gilpin executed several copies. Samuel Whitbread has kindly sent me a photograph of a different version Gilpin painted, in which the fox lies on its back and no humans are present at all – and the Courtauld Institute of Art has several other versions as well. The popularity of this scene underscores that eighteenth-century hunters found the kill as vital to their enjoyment as the 20-mile run leading up to it.

John Sidey and his Hounds at a Farmhouse near Hadleigh, Suffolk, by James Dunthorne, 1765, oil on canvas.

The excitement of the wild, hard ride in which almost anything might happen is caricatured in James Dunthorne's *John Sidey and his Hounds at a Farmhouse near Hadleigh* (1765). Although the event depicted supposedly happened in reality, the scene remains low comedy, of a piece with widespread satires of sportsmen's boorishness, indicating that at the start of the eighteenth century fox-hunting served as anything but the social ideal of gentlemanly behaviour.

Up through the Napoleonic wars, sportsmen were easily identified as the rural counterpart to the urban rake, for this was still the age when social status brought a man the privilege of indulging in drink, sex and violence with impunity. Tastes that would have been frowned upon, and punished, among the lower classes were encouraged among the upper.[7] Gilpin's commemorative scene, along with the 20-mile run and Thornton's order to have his hounds killed in order to serve as models, illustrates how the violent death became the necessary climax to the chase; there had to be a kill punctuating the hard ride. The exciting chase culminating in the death of the villainous fox became the emblem for the fast and loose way of life that wealth and class made possible. Fox-hunting, gambling, drinking and sex all became contests in which men competed against their fellows. And, from the 1790s until the Reform of 1832, the period when reactionary politics held sway, aristocratic gentlemen indulged themselves freely, distilling fox-hunting to an essence that persisted long after the violence and excess were eliminated.

Around 1780 one of the rakish young sportsmen, Childe Kinlet, known as the 'Flying Childe', made his mark by riding closely behind the hounds and jumping all the fences that came his way, setting the pattern of 'thrusting' imitated by other riders who otherwise probably would not have found an interest in fox-hunting. In 1787 Ralph Lambton joined these wealthy young men, and enjoyed the excitement so much that two years later he bought a house in what was then the tiny Leicestershire village of Melton Mowbray. Because this village proved to be extremely convenient for the Belvoir and Cottesmore, as well as the Quorn Hunt countries, it quickly became the popular residence for all the hunting gentlemen who rushed to make up the bold field of thrusters.

Accommodating this fashionable and fast set was the man who probably had the most obvious influence on the development of the sport, Hugo Meynell. As Master of the Quorn Hunt from 1753 to 1800, Meynell wielded the influence to develop what came to be known as the Meynellian system of fox-hunting. With two important innovations, he turned the sport from a slow woodland hunt into an exciting cross-country chase. It was he who bred the hounds that could run fast over long distances, and he who changed the traditional starting time of the hunt from dawn to mid-morning, arguing that foxes were more inclined to run later in the day when they had digested their food than in the earlier hours when they were sleepy after a night's hunting. This second change had the added benefit of enabling people to reach the hunt from beyond the local neighbourhood, and of allowing gentlemen to join in the hunt field without having to rise too early from their drink-sodden slumbers.

In contrast to Meynell, Peter Beckford argued for a different style of fox-hunting. In *Thoughts on Hunting* (1779), he asserted that 'the intemperance, clownishness, and ignorance of the old Fox-hunter, are quite worn out . . . Fox-hunting is now become the amusement of *gentlemen*; nor need any gentleman be ashamed of it.' With this pronouncement, Beckford tried to counteract the associations of the sport with rakish and violent behaviour, steering attention away from the exciting and dangerous rides sought by men like the Flying Childe, and emphasizing the technical aspects of the contest. But he also claimed that the most important consideration of fox-hunting was 'the

Richard Roper, *Hunter held by a Stable Boy*, 1762, oil on canvas.

killing of the fox', and the chase itself was less a form of entertainment than a discipline, resembling the successful battle: 'it should be short, sharp, and decisive'.[8] This attitude is depicted in Richard Roper's painting of 1762, *A Hunter Held by a Stableboy for his Master*, in which the static composition emphasizes the gentleman's dispassionate participation in venery, while the two fox skins nailed to the wall provide proof of the understanding that a disciplined hunt is nothing without a sure kill. In contrast, for thrusters like the Flying Childe, the fox's death provided the exciting culmination of a hard, dangerous ride.

In the first decades of the nineteenth century, the violent destruction of foxes began to stand out as the emblem of the seigneurial right of well-born men to indulge themselves in rakish – or boorish – fashion without recrimination. The Meynellian mode held sway, as men like George Osbaldeston and John Mytton epitomized the set of wealthy gambling men, notorious for their bibulism, rough speech and violent behaviour, who saw fox-hunting as a hard ride leading to the inevitable kill. 'Squire' Osbaldeston (1787–1866) – master at different times from the late 1810s through the early 1830s of the Quorn, the Pytchley and the Hambledon – once attacked a group of shoemakers who intruded into the Pytchley Hunt races, and on another occasion

Mr Holyoake, Mr Osbaldeston and Sir Harry Goodricke, an 1827 hunting piece by John Ferneley. Osbaldeston and others set the tone for rakish young thrusters in the early 19th century.

charged down a shepherd who protested against the loss of his sheep hurdles from the squire's rough riding. A heavy gambler, he lost nearly £200,000 on horse racing, destroying his once impressive income so that he was limited to wagers at the Portland Club of no more than one guinea an evening.[9] But while he was able, Squire Osbaldeston hunted hard and fast.

Jack Mytton, Master of the Albrighton from 1817 to 1821, was usually too drunk to hunt more than one fox a day, and is probably best remembered for attempting to cure his hiccups by setting his nightshirt on fire. Like Osbaldeston and Meynell, Mytton inherited an enormous fortune when he was still quite young. Expelled from Harrow for attacking his tutor, he proclaimed that he would attend university only if he never had to read anything other than the *Racing Calendar* and the *Stud Book*. He drank seven bottles of wine a day, advancing with maturity to an impressive seven bottles of brandy, and not only found a life for himself in the world of fox-hunting as a drunkard and a thug, but figured prominently enough to be the subject of an admiring biography. For him, fox-hunting provided only pleasure in its fast runs and dangerous jumps with a large, rowdy field. Not surprisingly, he died of alcoholic poisoning in debtors' prison. Osbaldeston's violence and Mytton's personal excesses were the outgrowth of the aristocratic rakishness expressed in the hard ride leading to the fox's gory death. Just as Colonel Thornton could cavalierly order his hounds to be killed so that Sawrey Gilpin could pose them, so thirty years later gentlemen still boasted of riding their horses to death.

The most prominent sports journalist of the day, Charles Apperley, who wrote under the pen-name 'Nimrod', promoted the fast riding, hard drinking and snobbery that had arisen from the Meynellian system, and at the same time placed great credence in the technical details of hunting as outlined by

Beckford. The series of articles that he began writing for the *Sporting Magazine* in 1822 attracted a large readership by describing aristocratic fox-hunters riding their horses furiously over farmers' fields and fences, and in using the increasingly technical jargon to make the hunt more of a serious and rule-bound performance of professionals than a free-for-all charge. As this image spread, the thruster became the recognized model of the fox-hunter, but one dressed according to strict rules, and well versed in the technical aspects of the hounds' work, of coverts and of farriery. Needless to say, the experiences of the sportsman that Nimrod idealized would have been inaccessible to most of the *Sporting Magazine*'s readers.

The inaccessibility of these ideals did not prevent non-aristocratic riders from emulating them, however. When Nimrod, who did not himself possess sufficient personal wealth to keep up with the fast set he portrayed, demanded that his editor cover his exorbitant expenses, he was summarily replaced by Robert Smith Surtees. In addition to going on to found the *New Sporting Magazine* in 1831, Surtees wrote a series of hunting novels featuring the greengrocer Jorrocks, who typifies the new kind of sportsman starting to appear around the time of the Reform Bill of 1832. This new hunting man was the non-aristocratic, middle-class person who had enough money to join a subscription pack – in which the members paid dues for the upkeep of the coverts, the training of the hounds and the mending of fences. In Surtees's novel of 1854, *Handley Cross; or, Mr Jorrocks's Hunt*, the action pivots around the collective decision by the town of Handley Cross to convert the pack of coursing hounds left at the death of Michael Hardey into a pack of foxhounds and to maintain them through subscription. No doubt attracted initially by the sensational riding and scandalous antics of the early squires, the middle-class fox-hunter, exemplified by the chubby Mr Jorrocks –

Frontispiece to R. S. Surtees, *Handley Cross* (1854). The picture shows Mr Jorrocks, a Cockney grocer become MFH, throttling a fox.

who speaks with a Cockney accent – became the mainstay of the sport for the rest of the century. While the aristocratic hunts of the Shires remained the cynosure of the hunting world, the less glamorous subscription hunts were more often than not the reality for most people of comfortable means. And with their new money, the middle-class sportsmen brought new attitudes towards the countryside, public behaviour and drinking.

Fox-hunting began to lose the martial focus that Beckford had assigned to it, as well as the associations with the violent rakishness of an exclusive class, and turned instead into the performative sign of membership in the respectable middle class. The kill was no longer necessary, as either the culmination of excitement or as proof of disciplined skills. The real meaning of the hunt now lay in the knowledge of how to dress, how to ride and jump, and how to use the correct terminology with the proper pronunciation. The kill remained, indeed, but only as the ostensible justification for the broader social event.

Already signs had appeared that, after the Napoleonic Wars, the emphasis on violence had begun to give way to the emphasis on the indicators of social accomplishment. In 1818, at the request of Lord Darlington, J.M.W. Turner painted *Raby Castle* depicting a hunt and posing the kill in the foreground, with the huntsman holding the dead fox aloft. But Darlington must have disliked the overt depiction of violence – and the painting was harshly criticized at the Royal Academy as the 'detestable fox hunting picture', so Turner painted over the scene to retain only the sedate view of the hunt field moving across the landscape.[10] The reaction to the first version of the painting was shaped by the fear that any direct association of an upper-class person with the violent conclusion of fox-hunting could be interpreted as an analogy of the heavy-handed oppression of the lower classes by the aristocracy. In the context of the social agitation in Britain after the wars, upper-class fox-hunters sought to downplay the violence. If painters thereafter depicted the kill, it was always in a way that made the actual event seem calm and respectable, reminding everyone that the fox was a villain whose destruction made a peaceful society possible. By the time that Surtees's imaginary town of Handley Cross had switched from coursing to fox-hunting, the glamour of the scarlet-coated hunt field had become the reason why people wanted to hunt: the kill remained necessary, but the energetic attention previously devoted to it was increasingly transferred to the technical details of participating properly in the field. It was this change, as much as the developments of horse, hound and landscape, that enabled the middle class to idealize fox-hunting nationalistically as an ancient tradition of the specifically English countryside.

Much of the change in attitude towards fox-hunting was generated by the artistic representations of the hunt and hunters. Even rather early painters like John Nost Sartorius promoted a

John Nost
Sartorius, *Death
of the Fox*,
c. 1805–10,
oil on canvas.

sedate view of hunting in scenes like *Death of the Fox*. On the one hand, this is a formulaic scene, with the huntsman holding the dead fox over his head to celebrate the kill and to help keep the hounds' blood up; the two members of the hunt field on the left strike the standard pose of pointing to the dead fox with their whips and praising one another for being present at the kill. But even as a death, the scene assures us that fox-hunting helps to stabilize the countryside. The fox itself is not mangled; the violence of Gainsborough's and Gilpin's scenes has been wholly extricated since the action is not of the hounds swarming in on the fox but of the hunt successfully concluded with the pack obediently holding back. The woman leaning out of the upstairs window seems to be welcoming the hunt, relieved at being freed from the hen-stealing Reynard. The leafy trees surrounding the cottages and the warm lighting of the painting make this into a comfortable, pleasant setting where fox-hunting preserves the English countryside along with its traditions, as represented in the thatched cottages, picket fences and welcoming people.

Fox-hunting scenes followed in quantity throughout the nineteenth century, appearing in series of three or four paintings, demarcating the main stages of the hunt, such as *The Meet*, *Breaking Covert*, *The Chase* and *The Kill*. These series became common fare among sporting artists, and often depict a particular chase on a specific day or a particular hunt with its notable members. Numerous painters produced series of this sort, though probably the best known was Henry Alken, who painted from 1813 to 1850. His works frequently complemented Nimrod's articles in the *Sporting Magazine*, and have graced the walls of countless pubs, inns and even schoolrooms. Alken's paintings set the standard for later illustrations of the hunt, both in arranging the scenes as serial narratives and in emphasizing the details of tack and clothing to make the chase into a social function adhering to specific rules.

It would be impossible to offer more than a single representation of a hunt series because so many artists published numerous examples: according to Stella Walker, a count of works by Henry Alken alone was halted 'in despair when five figures was reached'.[11] One such work stands out for its sophistication, however, the rather late series by George Goodwin Kilburne, *The Cheshire Hunt* (*c*. 1900). By the time these scenes were published, hunt series had established strong conventions that artists could exploit in the depiction of highly social events. *The Cheshire Hunt* is classified as sport painting because of its depiction of the hunt,

George Kilburne, *Cheshire Hunt: The Kill at Peckforton Hills*, c. 1900, oil on canvas.

and its progression through the standard – even ritualistic – phases: *The Meet at Caverly Hall, Breaking Cover, Full Cry: Making for the Peckforton Hills* and *The Kill at Peckforton*.

Kilburne exploited the genre of hunting scenes in order to depict the interactions among different classes, animals and the landscape. The fact that he did not usually work in the sporting genre makes these hunt scenes all the more representative in showing how firmly established the conventions of hunting series had become that a non-sporting, mainstream painter could execute a series with complete mastery. What is most notable about Kilburne's scenes – though it is easily forgotten in the excitement and the sophistication of the narrative – is that there is no fox. This dramatic work of visual reportage captures the polished and stately progression of the hunt, from the meet at the manor, to the chase, to the kill, and in each scene the attention is given over entirely to the field itself, the fox lying beyond the frame of each painting. The kill occurs at such a distance in the final scene that the title serves only as the conventional closing of such a hunt series. Although there is a good deal of drama, it is all directed to displaying how hunting socializes the countryside for the benefit of all, not just a few indulged men.

The wide proliferation of series like *The Cheshire Hunt*, with their adherence to the generic format, created the sense that fox-hunting followed a definite and repeatable progression, constituted by clearly delimited phases, towards a decisive conclusion: the success of a particular hunt could be measured by how closely it approximated the representative ideal. The people who wanted to belong to the society depicted in the scenes had to dress properly; their horses had to be groomed adequately and had to perform athletically; the hounds had to fulfil their tasks enthusiastically; the countryside had to provide fast gallops and challenging jumps; and the fox had to break covert, give a good chase and be killed. The set form of these series helped to affirm the notion that fox-hunting had attained a professional status, and that it upheld a natural – because infinitely repeatable – rhythm of meet, chase, kill.

Hounds and riders of the West Grinstead and Horsham Hunt, September 2004.

After 1850 the hunt field was dominated by high-handedly moral men like George Whyte-Melville and Anthony Trollope. These were the men who idealized fox-hunting for bringing out the purest elements of 'manliness', understood in Whyte-Melville's terms as 'a moral quality, the result of education, sentiment, self-respect, and certain high aspirations of the intellect'.[12] This high-handedness moved fox-hunting away from the drinking, swearing and gambling that had characterized the earlier decades, but it continued to cast the fox as vermin, whose eradication would be a service to the countryside. But since, as is evident in *The Cheshire Hunt*, respectable ladies had also become more frequent among the hunt field, even less emphasis was placed on the violence of the fox's death. As the ethos of fox-hunting changed from rogues chasing a rogue to gentlefolk upholding the morality of the nation, descriptions of the sport moved away from the sensationalist journalism of Nimrod and into middle-class novels like those of Anthony Trollope.

In *The Eustace Diamonds* of 1871, Trollope (himself a thruster, but so near-sighted that he seldom saw what he jumped) makes use of a fox-hunt to display his characters' concerns about money, social prestige and their ability to meet class expectations. Lizzie Eustace, a young widow who has to struggle to hold onto her wealth and social position, strategically hosts a hunting party to establish her place within polite society. Secretly, Lizzie worries about her newly learned riding skills and that a fall will knock out her front teeth, but once the hunt begins, she forgets her fears of physical injury and begins to see the chase as a contest with another young woman whom she envies, Lucinda Roanoke:

> [Lizzie] thought that she was getting nearer to Lucinda. For her, in her heart, Lucinda was the quarry. If she could only pass Lucinda! That there were any hounds she had

altogether forgotten . . . She knew she was gaining a little, because she could see how well and squarely Lucinda sat upon her horse . . . 'Oh, if I could do it like that!' thought Lizzie. But in that very minute she was doing it, not only as well but better.[13]

Throughout this episode Trollope focuses on the social aspects of the hunt field, emphasizing the qualities that distinguish his characters against the backdrop of the natural landscape over which they possess proprietary rights. No one acts scandalously, and everyone stays completely sober. And not only are ladies present in the field: Lizzie is the premier member, even providing the focus of the narrative to show how a social climber can assert her proprietorship over the countryside as though she were born to it. Most importantly, foxes do not even matter in this narrative, since the real quarry is Lizzie's social rival, Lucinda Roanoke: the kill has ceased to reflect the violence of the hunt field, because it has disappeared behind the middle class's image of itself as the natural proprietor of the peaceful countryside.

By the end of the nineteenth century fox-hunting had so successfully instituted the mythic view of itself into the British national ethos that Siegfried Sassoon could use it in *Memoirs of a Fox-Hunting Man* to embody what was lost in the Great War. Casting himself as George Sherston, Sassoon portrays with astonishing acuity the pre-war world of the Tory countryside, where a young man with little ambition can give his life focus by going from hunting season to cricketing season and back again. Although little given to reflection, Sherston holds a deep appreciation for nature, as shown in his account of cub-hunting – the springtime work when the young members of the pack are trained to kill foxes (for the hounds have no natural animosity towards or appetite for their victims) by encouraging them to tear apart young fox cubs: 'The crunch of delving spades and the smell of sandy soil now mingled with the redolence of the perspiring pack, the crushed bracken that the horses were munching, and the pungent, unmistakable odour of foxes. However inhumane its purpose, it was a kindly country scene.'[14] Sassoon's genius – and unflinching honesty – comes in that final, jarring sentence that has Sherston paying mild lip service to the cruelty of cub-hunting precisely in order to overshadow it with the more important feeling for the kindness of the country scene.

When Sherston first joins the fight in France, he is proud that his identity as a fox-hunter helps him advance, by 'being able to converse convincingly about hunting' with the better officers: 'It gave one an almost unfair advantage in many ways.' But as more of his fellow fox-hunting officers die, Sherston begins to feel that the war holds less connection to that 'kindly country scene' where he had learnt to conduct himself well while being inhumane. Finally he admits to himself, 'I begin to see that the War has re-made me and done away with a lot of my ideas that were no good.'[15] The system that made the fox-hunting man into an ideal Englishman has disappeared, for, surrounded by devastation, Sherston can no longer look away from the kill.

After the First World War and throughout the twentieth century into the twenty-first, apologists of fox-hunting have become increasingly urgent in their assertions that the sport somehow embodies the full history of the British Isles. Like Sassoon, they understand that the end of fox-hunting would signal the end of the class system of privilege. Correspondingly, opponents of fox-hunting know that their greatest weapon against the pro-hunting lobby lies in reminding the public of the violence of the kill. Photographs of mangled fox corpses are published by anti-hunting groups to de-sublimate the kill so

Hounds of the Royal Artillery Hunt killing their fox after a 'successful' hunt, the last before the hunting ban, introduced in Britain on 18 February 2005.

that the fox ceases to be Reynard the thief, noxious embodiment of anti-Englishness, and becomes an animal tormented by people seeking to uphold the fantasy of 'a kindly country scene'.

The view that fox-hunting provides a service to the rural communities is obviated by the fact that throughout the nineteenth century the fox population was artificially maintained to satisfy the need of fox-hunters. Brian Vesey-Fitzgerald asserts 'that at the end of the eighteenth century and in the early years of the nineteenth, the fox, from the Highlands of Scotland to the coast of Hampshire was nowhere really plentiful'.[16] Along with certain environmental factors, throughout the centuries bounties paid on foxes to help preserve domestic fowl had kept the English vulpine population in check. By the time the foxhound and hunter had been developed, and by the time enclosures had created a countryside conducive to exciting chases, the fox itself was already scarce in England.

Nowadays the fox population in England remains steady, and apologists of fox-hunting often claim that it is hunting that preserves the fox. Charlie Pye-Smith quotes John Waldron, a Wiltshire farmer, as saying: 'we farmers only put up with the fox for the hunting. If they stop us hunting, I think they would be exterminated. It'd be the easiest thing in the world to wipe out the fox population.'[17] Given the difficulty that other nations have had in eradicating red foxes, Mr Waldron's boast does not hold much weight, but it does reflect one of the central ways that fox-hunting has shaped the relations between foxes and humans, for fox-hunters have made vulpicide – the killing of foxes by non-hunters – into one of the most serious crimes in the countryside.

Technically, because foxes have never been protected by Game Laws, vulpicide was legal, although, as Vesey-Fitzgerald says: 'it was the most heinous of all sins'.[18] That killing a fox outside the hunt could be proclaimed a sin indicates how much of an institution fox-hunting had become in the countryside. Writing two hundred years after Peter Beckford, the 10th Duke of Beaufort, asserts that 'no one who hunts seriously is interested in the actual kill'.[19] The dukes of Beaufort have always played a central role in English fox-hunting, and indeed it was the 8th Duke who established the Masters of Fox Hounds Association in 1881. The 10th Duke's pointed sublimation of the kill is intended to refute anti-hunting propaganda by emphasizing the professional demands, such as the management of the hounds, the technical requirements of riding well, and the close bond between fox-hunting and the natural rhythms of the countryside.

Hunt balls and breakfasts, sartorial codes and jargon all provide the means for participants to prove their adherence to values that supposedly are as ancient as nature itself. These details, along with the standards for the performance of the hounds and riders, justify Beaufort's belittlement of the kill as the primary reason for the hunt. And certainly it is in the ability to participate knowledgeably in the peripheral matters that the prestige of hunting lies. As in Lizzie Eustace's experience, it is in dressing properly, riding well, pronouncing 'covert' correctly that someone proves they are a fox-hunter, and consequently that they belong to the society rooted in the countryside that defines England.

A fox's carcass is flung into the air for the pack after 'A Kill with the New Forest Foxhounds'. From a 1920s book on fox-hunting.

Fox-hunting is an artificially structured activity in a landscape that has also been artificially shaped; foxhounds have been genetically engineered through careful breeding to create a canine suited to one purpose; thoroughbreds similarly have been bred specifically to keep up with the swifter foxhounds. The culture surrounding the actual hunt – such as dress, terminology and protocol for riding – is accordingly highly ritualistic. As Garry Marvin indicates, the hunt still serves as the ritual trial where the fox, indicted as an outlaw, has the right to prove itself.[20] But the contest, or trial, in which the fox mostly loses,

In November 2004 a fox joined the hounds of the Dulverton West Hunt on Exmoor. It ran among the hounds unnoticed before making its get-away through a gap in the hedge.

has become one in which the fox remains almost invisible. A strong suggestion in Marvin's studies is that if the fox were thought of more as a legitimate participant in the natural world, instead of a thief who must be punished, the complex culture of fox-hunting would not be possible.

And yet, even though the fox has been sublimated into near invisibility, it cannot be eliminated from the hunt. Drag hunting, in which a person is selected to serve as the 'fox' and drag a burlap sack saturated with a scent to attract the hounds, is generally held in low regard. Of course, the person who plays 'fox' can lay a complex line for the hounds to work, and provide as much excitement for both those who enjoy watching the hounds and those who enjoy jumping over fences as if a real fox were being chased for its life. But with no fox at the end of the line, and no chance for a real kill that would eliminate an outlaw, a drag hunt is little more than a dress rehearsal, and makes the artificiality of the entire fox-hunting enterprise too obvious. In chasing hounds that are pursuing a line leading to no kill, the human participants cannot avoid recognizing that fox-hunting is merely an institution developed to make their social activity *appear* natural. Only the fox can make the illusion work.

In the current debate over fox-hunting, the role of the fox is still in dispute. Vesey-Fitzgerald observes that the 'positively enormous hunting literature' usually makes only 'passing reference to the fox, the fount of it all'.[21] Donna Landry complements this observation when she points out the limitations of those less sympathetic to hunting than she is: 'identification with dogs rather than with birds, hares, or foxes is an aspect of the culture of field sports often ignored'.[22] And even though the fox was once declared one of the three most important animals in Britain, fox-hunting depends on the low esteem in which the animal is held. Not only the kill, but the trade in bagged foxes, the practice of the cubbing season and the boasts of farmers like the archetypal Mr Waldron reiterate how low the fox ranks in the range of sympathy that humans customarily extend to animals. And, indeed, as the Labour government has finally succeeded in banning fox-hunting in England, their intention is not to save the foxes but rather to realign control over the countryside. Just

'Jack Rogers putting his Nerves to Right', 19th-century print. The social activities surrounding the hunt eventually overshadowed the fox itself.

Tableau of boar and foxes.

as Oliver Cromwell's soldiers slaughtered the king's stags in order to end royalist control over the land, so Labour has again stymied the aristocratic regulation of the landscape through the institution of fox-hunting. The ban passed in February 2005 came as the culmination of a centuries-long class conflict that included numerous laws restricting who can hunt, who can own dogs and guns, and who possesses access to the land. If the Roman Cerialia saw the burning of foxes as the means of arousing the fertile power of the earth, so, ironically, English fox-hunting, with its complex history of bourgeois appropriation and parliamentary regulation, extends the belief that the source of powers – both generative and wicked – lies in the earth.

5 The Commercial Fox

As the fox disappeared behind the social rituals of English fox-hunting, it acquired a commercial value that – as an animal that refuses to be domesticated – it had not previously had. When foxes were bought and sold as bagmen to supply the English hunt, they acquired a positive economic value for possibly the first time. And at almost the same historical moment that the fox changed from the valueless vermin to Charlie, it also acquired a commercial value for its fur. But longer-standing associations have also persisted as advertising campaigns capitalize on fox images that combine the older Reynard associations with the nineteenth-century Charlie Fox character to sell a diverse range of non-vulpine products. Although some species of fox are eaten by people, and some are sold as pets, the fox generally resists cul-turation. Its economic values still reflect the biases contained in the stories we tell, epithets assigned to people and actions, and that preserve social institutions like fox-hunting.

The commerce in bagged foxes proved controversial even in the early days because the imported fox too often failed to provide a good run, not knowing the lie of the land where it suddenly found itself pursued by hounds with their blood up. Surtees called the bagged fox a 'short running dastardly traitor', emphasizing that in committing the crime of being killed too quickly the fox let down the entire hunt field by failing to play

Many hunting ornaments wittily depict the fox as one of the field. Here Charlie Fox relaxes after a good run, reminiscing over the days before animal rights activists and socialists took over the country.

its proper role.[1] French foxes in particular were derided as being degenerate, and a serious threat to the native sturdiness of the English foxhound. But the controversy over foreign influence obscured a curiosity of the trade in 'bagmen', namely that an inedible animal should become a consumable product. For the sole product being consumed in the bagmen trade was the fox's death, which was already being hidden from view by the hunting institution. The value lay in the death, not the animal itself, and since foxes were officially classified in the Game Laws as vermin, they received none of the concern directed towards other species by the growing animal rights movements.

From the European continent, foxes were shipped in small rabbit cages aboard cattle ships. In Leadenhall Market in London they were sold for 10 to 15 shillings apiece, a sizeable enough sum to indicate their demand by fox-hunters. Squire Osbaldeston had a standing order for six foxes per week – a necessity since the farmers within the area of his hunt expressed their dislike of him by committing the sin of vulpicide on a large scale.[2] All of a sudden, with the market in imported foxes, the animal that had been held in low esteem, classified at the bottom of the natural hierarchy, acquired a new value measured by the demand reflected in the high price. Previously the fox had fetched a bounty paid within the local parish to keep its numbers down, and to protect farmers' chickens and geese. Payment of a bounty actually signified a negative value for the fox itself, reflecting the higher value of the farmyard fowl that the fox was being killed to protect. When fox-hunters needed the fox to perpetuate their sport, the animal acquired a positive commercial value, but one that was still attached only to its death.

The Burns Report, commissioned in 2000 by the British government to study the economic role of fox-hunting in the countryside in order to understand the effects of a ban on hunting, estimates that the vulpine population in England keeps at a

Caged silver foxes in a Chinese meat market, 2003.

stable 250,000, with between 21,000 and 25,000 foxes killed every year by both traditional hunts with horses and hounds and foot hunts, where foxes are chased by hounds towards a row of people with shotguns.[3] By factoring in the cost of maintaining coverts, keeping horses and hounds, along with all the other expenses of hunting, the Burns Report calculates that each fox killed in England costs an average of £930.[4] The hunting lobby would argue that the 'price' is skewed, since it actually reflects the social values of maintaining the countryside traditions, and that the fox itself holds no value. In fact, these traditions have all arisen to conceal the fox's death.

When the fox acquires commercial value for something other than dying, it is usually for the roguish character held over from the Reynard tradition, which consumers become quickly fond of. Advertisers for Old Speckled Hen Ale, for example, exploit the rakishly distinguished aspect of the fox character in a major ad campaign: the fox proverbially lusting for a chicken dinner is no different than we are when, after a long, dry day, we crave to

'When it comes to a Hen, I'm always first in the pecking order', says the thirsty fox ordering a pint of Morland's Old Speckled Hen.

slake our thirst with a pint of Old Speckled Hen. The delightful
advertising ploy of the fox commenting on the joy of 'catching a
hen' has the effect of making all thirsty beer lovers into foxes.
These commercials dress up a fox into a gentleman beer lover,
with the joke being considerably less brutal, since the 'hen' is a
delectable and life-giving potation. The beer invites consumers
to take on a foxy character, and this one in a role recognizable
from a cultural tradition that bypasses fox-hunting. Old
Speckled Hen recovers the European image of the charming,
sexy rogue, Reynard, in stark contrast to the felonious villain of
the hunting ritual.

Plenty of brand names include fox logos, consisting of the
distinctive fox head, as in Fox Racing Equipment, or displaying
a running fox, as in Fox Photo Labs. In the 1970s Audi introduced a car in North America called the Fox, which took its
place alongside numerous other cars with animal names, such
as the Mustang, Impala and Beetle. Ostensibly, Audi's Fox was
so branded because, unlike most American cars of the time, it

was swift and agile. The name enabled owners to signify their own swift and agile intelligence, in contrast to the muscular Mustang or the hideously cute Beetle, but it also reflected the cunning of marketing, for in America Audi had traditionally been an expensive luxury car, and the Audi Fox was advertised as a luxury car that was affordable to middle-income buyers. People could have the prestige of the expensive imported nameplate, Audi, without having to pay top dollar. The car proved to be a cunning fox in convincing buyers that they had acquired much more than in fact they had, since the car was actually a basic model. Animal names for cars have ostensibly provided drivers with a way to express some primal quality of themselves, and the Audi Fox enabled drivers to feel that they bore the character of the roguishly sophisticated fox, since European cars were far less common in America in the 1970s than now.

Apart from fox images, the most extensive commercialization of the fox came with the fur market, which exploded about the same time as the rise of fox-hunting. Before the mid-eighteenth century, few people in western Europe wore fur, since it was associated with barbarian clothing. In 1785 Thomas Gainsborough painted a portrait of Sarah Siddons with a fox-fur muff and a fur-trimmed mantle, indicating that fur had by then found a place in Western fashion. Gainsborough seems to have intended his portrait of the famous actress as a corrective to Sir Joshua Reynolds's hyperbolic depiction of her as *The Tragic Muse*, by painting her as she actually dressed – in the height of fashion.[5] As one of the most famous women of her day, Mrs Siddons represented much of what was understood as womanhood, and her costume would provide a measure for what other women would wear if they aspired to approximate her quality.

In the mid-eighteenth-century, just prior to Mrs Siddons's portrait, foxes began to be commercialized for their fur. Aileen

Mrs Sarah Siddons by Thomas Gainsborough, 1785, oil on canvas. The popular actress accentuated her fashionable dress with red fox fur.

Ribeiro lists numerous fashion trends throughout Europe that have included fur over the past three centuries, the most dramatic being the full coat or cape – the pelisse, which by the early nineteenth century had evolved into a close-fitting sleeved coat sometimes lined with fur. Napoleon's wife, Empress Josephine, favoured a pelisse lined with 'golden fox'.[6] In 1777 Gustavus III of Sweden received a blue fox pelisse from Catherine the Great of Russia, a gift intended to express the giver's wealth and power.[7]

Paintings from the eighteenth century of wealthy people wearing fur generally refer to the person's travels, but fur was used rarely in western Europe on the outside of garments, appearing mostly as the lining to coats and mantles, and as the increasingly ubiquitous trim. Fashionable people from the period

Elizabeth Farren, 1790, oil on canvas. This portrait by Thomas Lawrence emphasizes the broad range of the actress by contrasting the texture of the fox fur with her hair.

used fur to create a sense both of complexity and of exoticism to their wardrobe that made them appealing. Like the portrait of Sara Siddons, that of Eliza Farren, also a popular actress, employs a fur muff and cape to contrast with her hair. The dramatic background adds to the sense that the woman holding the fur is capable of considerable passion, even though her mild facial expression makes her seem temperate. These contrasts in textures and moods suggest that this is an actress of considerable range, a woman who may portray innocence as well as barbaric savagery. This range is indicated not only by the stormy sky, but the fox fur, which, according to Ribeiro, 'was made popular by the involvement of the central European troops – and in particular the Hungarian hussars with their glamorous, fur-lined uniforms of Oriental origin – in the War of the Austrian Succession which began in 1740'.[8]

One hundred and eighty years after Gainsborough painted Sarah Siddons's portrait, Marilyn Monroe appeared on the cover of *Life* magazine in an Arctic fox-fur hat and collar. In this portrait, the fox serves the opposite purpose that it did for either Sara Siddons or Eliza Farren, for the white fur in the *Life* picture complements Marilyn Monroe's platinum hair and blue

Life magazine cover of Marilyn Monroe in Arctic fox fur, 1962.

eyes, poignantly subduing the sexual associations that the 'Blonde Bombshell' – who had died only shortly before the cover appeared – had otherwise acquired. Thanks to the fur of the Arctic fox, the woman whose boldness had made her into a sexual icon appears surprisingly vulnerable in this picture.

Once the fashion for fur took hold in the nineteenth century, an industry developed to supply the demand, with large fortunes being made by trapping foxes in the Pacific Northwest. Because trappers always faced the threat of diminishing returns, they sought to guarantee a constant source of furs by introducing Arctic foxes onto Alaskan islands. When the explorer Vitus Bering arrived in Alaska in 1741, almost all the islands in the Aleutian chain, as well as in the Alaskan Peninsula and in the Gulf of Alaska, were free of any fox species.[9] In 1750 Russian trappers captured some Arctic foxes from the Commander Islands in the Bering Sea, and released them further south on Attu, the westernmost island in the Aleutian Chain, thereby ensuring a steady supply of foxes to trap within a restricted range. Throughout the nineteenth century Russian trappers released Arctic foxes, as well as red foxes, on an increasing number of Aleutian Islands, so that by the 1930s more than 450 of the islands had been stocked with foxes specifically for the purpose of supplying the fur trade. The trappers found this strategy highly effective, because the islands were the home of many small animals common to fox diets, enabling the foxes to flourish without having to be fed by the trappers. Even more than this, the islands also provided natural barriers to migration, ensuring that the foxes brought to an island would stay there. In effect, the islands served as giant cages, which is why foxes were introduced only on the southernmost islands, since these remained free of the winter ice that could provide a means of escape – many of the northern islands of the Bering Sea, such as the Commander Islands, in fact, have an indigenous population of foxes simply because of the possible connection with the mainland during the winter. So successful was this strategy of using islands as cages that the United States government – always a closer friend to business than to ecological sustainability – officially began to lease the islands in 1882 specifically for that purpose.

The motive behind finding more efficient means of maintaining the supply of foxes is straightforward. Records of the Hudson Bay Company show that Arctic fox pelts fetched the highest price for any fur throughout the nineteenth century; although beaver pelts held first place in volume, they had only one quarter the value of blue-phase Arctic fox skins. These high prices led to a serious decline in the fox population throughout Canada, driving efforts to find a viable means of raising foxes in captivity, all of which failed before 1890.

In 1883 Charles Dalton of Prince Edward Island, Canada, paid $100 for a pair of dark Arctic foxes that had been dug out of the ground by a farmer. From this pair Dalton got two litters in successive years, which established his breeding stock. Since he observed that pairs would breed for only two seasons and then stop, he deduced that it was 'necessary to ranch them as nearly as possible to their natural conditions'.[10] In 1890 Robert Oulton joined forces with Dalton when he worked out that 'ranching' foxes in simulated natural conditions could be achieved by adding hollow logs to the pens so that the foxes could build nests. By 1913 fox farms following the strategy of Dalton and Oulton had spread to the western provinces of Canada and to the United States, and were finding welcome in other countries such as Russia, Japan, Denmark, Norway and Finland (where half of all Arctic fox-fur farms are now located)[11] – all started with Canadian breeding stock.

Photo of Charles Dalton holding his breeding foxes. By learning how to breed foxes in captivity, men like Dalton made a fortune selling high volumes of furs.

Caged foxes and raccoons in a village fur farm, Linyu, China, 2005. The Cuiwang Fur Company processes and sells all kinds of fur, including fox, silver fox, raccoon, leopard, cat and rabbit.

Woman wearing fox furs, *c.* 1911. By the time of the First World War, no fashion-conscious woman could leave home without her fox-fur neckpiece.

In the early twentieth century the biggest boon to the fox-fur industry came from the ladies' fashion for whole fox neckpieces. This fashion became so popular – and so lucrative for the fox-fur industry – that in June 1915 the *Fur Trade Review* expressed its gratitude with a jingle:

The summer girls are wrapped in fox
Of colour that becomes their locks;
And though the stones melt 'neath their feet,
They say they do not mind the heat.[12]

By the 1920s the fur companies – like the Semide
Propagating Company – had become among the most
profitable businesses in Alaska, behind only fishing and min-
ing. Nearly 400 fox farms were operating in 1925 throughout
the Alaskan Islands, with more than 36,000 foxes. And the
profits were impressive: in Alaska an Arctic fox skin would sell
for $150, and by the time it reached London would fetch
$2,800. Across Canada an average of 40,000 Arctic foxes have
been killed each year since 1919, with the number some years
reaching as high as 85,000. In Siberia as many as 100,000
Arctic fox skins have been sold in a year, though the numbers
have declined since 1989. According to the International Fur
Trade Federation (IFTF), 13 per cent of all pelts taken in 2002
were from foxes; that amounts to 4,615,000 skins.[13]

Confiscated
red fox skins,
in a US Fish and
Wildlife Service
law enforcement
photograph.

Similar trade in the skin or feathers of other animals has resulted in the extinction of entire species, but not so with either the Arctic or the red fox. Although several fox species – such as the South American *chilla* – have become endangered through over-hunting, red foxes and Arctic foxes have not. This is not to say that artificial fox populations had no broader impact, however, for the ecological effect of introducing non-indigenous foxes to the Alaskan islands began to appear quite early. By the early 1800s native bird populations had started to disappear; this was first noticed by the Aleut people, who had relied on the birds for food and clothing. The Aleutian Canada Goose became extinct on all but three of the smaller islands, and the seabirds – especially burrow-nesting varieties – that had bred on the rocky islands became seriously threatened. Because the trappers valued the birds only as food for the foxes, they gave little thought to ecological details such as the extinction of non-commercial animals. Where native populations of red foxes existed, such as on the Unalga and Ugamak Islands, the trappers took pains to eliminate them – since red fox fur has always fetched a lower price – in order to provide a niche for the Arctic fox.

In the Great Depression of the 1930s, the fur market collapsed, losing 50 per cent of its value in the single year of 1931. Trappers then destroyed as many of the fox populations throughout the islands as they could, through the traditional method of spring traps as well as poisoned bait. Bailey estimates that only 10 per cent of the Bering Sea islands on which foxes have been introduced since the mid-eighteenth century still contain members of either the *V. vulpes* or *Alopex* species.[14] Where the foxes have been destroyed, the bird populations have increased.

Although the Great Depression dealt the fur trade a serious blow, it still remained prosperous when compared to other forms of agriculture, due entirely to the technique of the fur farm. Fox-

Model wearing fox fur, Paris Fashion Week, 2001. Despite the efforts of anti-fur campaigns, many people continue to include fox fur in their fashion statements, often buying what they believe to be fake fur.

fur farms, following the strategies developed by Dalton and Oulton, proved so successful in sustaining a supply of breeding foxes and pelts that breeders began to put them to use in raising other fur-bearing animals, particularly mink, which proved especially lucrative, rising steadily in popularity. In the winter of 1939–40 sales of mink pelts surpassed those of fox for the first time, and have remained the highest-selling fur ever since.[15]

Eighty per cent of all fur now marketed comes from fur farms where the animals live crowded together in small wire cages. The description of farm conditions provided by the IFTF is probably accurate in itself. The Federation, which was organized to promote fur farming, says that foxes – as well as mink – 'are generally housed in sheds four metres wide. These sheds are open-sided with roofing panels. They provide normal temperature and light conditions, while protecting against direct sunlight, wind and rain. Wire cages are placed in rows in the sheds . . . the cages are raised off the ground to ensure good hygiene.' The account goes on to say that the animals 'are fed on a wet feed made from fish, dairy, poultry and other agricultural by-products'.[16] What this description leaves unstated is that within the wide, roomy sheds, the cages that actually confine the animals measure one square metre or less. And the description of the food mentions that it consists of a variety of 'agricultural by-products', which is a catch-all term for anything left over from food production. Fish and poultry by-products could, for example, mean scales and feathers, and the 'other agricultural by-products' could include the carcasses of the foxes' cage-mates who had already been skinned or who died prematurely through disease.

No animal can give up its skin without dying in the process. Fur 'farmers' insist that after the foxes have lived a few happy and inquisitive years in wire cages they are killed humanely. Most often the foxes are electrocuted, with one electrode clipped to their ear or nose and another pushed into their anus. Compared to the slow death of the leg-hold trap – which is now banned for its inherent cruelty in 60 countries around the world, but not in the United States – anal electrocution might be thought 'humane'. Or it might be considered 'humane' that electrocution puts an end to a miserable life. But when we recall

Photo of a fur
fox undergoing
electrocution.

that on these 'farms' foxes are born into small wire cages, where they eat the refuse of other industrialized 'farms' until their fur has attained the desired density, and are then electrocuted, it is a bit difficult to say honestly that any part of the process is 'humane'. Farmed foxes live miserably so that their killers may say that their death is humane.

The fox's ability to sustain the species through a high reproductive rate has proved a boon to the fur trade. Fox fur has become so cheap that it has replaced imitation fur, and is sometimes even sold as fake fur. Ninety per cent of fox fur from industrial 'farms' goes into fur trim on collars, boots and in the linings of gloves. In addition, the fur is often dyed so that it is not even distinguishable as the skin of a red fox. These practices have ensured once again that the fox remains ubiquitous in our lives; and the success of the fur trade has depended – just as with the fox-hunting institution – on concealing the death of the fox.

Opponents of fur sales follow the same strategy used by the people protesting against fox-hunting – of repeatedly publishing photos that make uncomfortably plain the grotesqueness of fur farming: if we consumers are kept from turning away from the death (and from the agonizing lives of farmed foxes), the

A silver-black fox carcass being stripped for fur in a Siberian fur farm, 2005.

artificiality of our bourgeois lives becomes discomfiting. In the same way, then, People for the Ethical Treatment of Animals (PETA) published a photograph as part of an anti-fur campaign that shows the singer Sophie Ellis-Bextor holding a dead fox by the forepaws, its head hanging limply. Ellis-Bextor strikes a fashion-plate pose in a disconcerting contrast to the dead fox she is holding: her dress, make-up and stance all compel us to want to see her glamorously wearing the fur that she is holding and that is still attached to the animal to which it belongs. And in forcing us to see the dead animal – since, after all, the photo-

A 2002 poster for PETA (People for the Ethical Treatment of Animals), a worldwide pressure-group, featuring the singer Sophie Ellis-Bextor revealing what happens to 'the rest of your fur coat'.

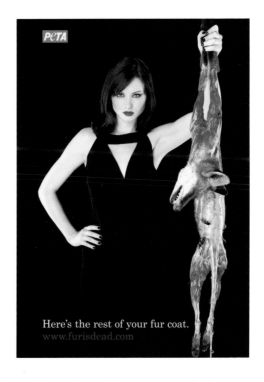

PeTA

Here's the rest of your fur coat.
www.furisdead.com

graph would have been alluring or cute if Ellis-Bextor were cuddling a live fox – we cannot help but remember that our fur coat, fur beret and fur-lined gloves all require the death that the fur trade conceals. This advertisement by PETA works by using the strategy that the fur trade must also rely upon to make fur appealing. The attractive woman – we should say the foxy lady – with the fur coat convinces women that they too can be foxy if they wear a coat. But Ellis-Bextor's picture confronts us with the truth that we would have to take the skin from a dead animal to be sexy. PETA's advertising campaign succeeds by exploiting the glossy images to reveal what advertising usually hides.

Julia Emberley adds a perspective on the debate over fur that complicates it beyond the dichotomy of the green anti-fur and land-use rights opposition by pointing out the roles that fur has played among Northern native peoples such as the Inuit and Dede. For indigenous people, she says, 'fur trapping represents one means of material support, as well as a symbolic tie to traditional ways of life, in an otherwise poverty-inducing economic system'.[17] Boycotts of fur by environmentally minded consumers have tended to overlook the impact of their politics on native communities that rely heavily on trapping for revenue. As long as Northern tribes could sustain cash profits from fur, they could continue their traditional cultures, which were centred on fishing, hunting and trapping. But with the fur market threatened by anti-fur lobbyists, these people have had to find jobs unrelated to any aspect of indigenous culture.[18] Emberly's insight is that the bourgeois commercialization of fur has had the odd effect of preserving cultures from complete capitalist exploitation and assimilation by exploiting them only partially. Like those arguing that a ban on fox-hunting would imperil the countryside economy, Emberly pits the preservation of animals against the preservation of people and culture. Her ability – and willingness – to create that opposition depends wholly on the low status of the fox.

Much of the defence of the fur industry, as well as the hunting institution, focuses on the fox as a pest, and indeed foxes often play a negative commercial role in undermining the success of agricultural reforms. As a predator, the fox is first pointed to by people as a threat to their livelihood, the vermin that steals the poultry that could be laying eggs and eventually ending up in the farmer's pot. In Argentina the *culpeo* had once been mostly ignored, since its tendency not to run away from humans meant that it had little value to sportsmen. But around

1915 ranchers began to increase their flocks of sheep, at which time the *culpeo* – which, unlike the much smaller red fox, is large enough to drag away a lamb – suddenly came to be considered a pest.[19] The Argentine situation exemplifies the way that commercial interests assign value – positive and negative – to animals. The *culpeo* offered no sport, and was therefore ignored, until people began importing the lambs that provided an irresistible temptation to the predators, at which point the *culpeo* acquired the negative value that the red fox had once known in England by having a bounty placed on it. Predators like the *culpeo* and the red fox acquire their negative value in competing with people for the same food. And as our competitors, as pests, foxes generally lie outside culinary tastes; but this has not always been so, nor is it with non-scented species.

The Neolithic dwellers among the alpine lakes of Switzerland left plenty of remains indicating that red foxes constituted at least part of their diet. Cut marks on fox bones found among the ancient dwellings prove that the flesh had been cut away and even gnawed off by human teeth.[20] Because of the strong odour retained in fox flesh, however, few people of more recent eras – excepting Roger Scruton, of course – have found it palatable.

In the regions of the world where red foxes give way to other, less strongly scented species, people have customarily found sources of food in the fox. The Arctic fox has provided in two ways for the local people, who watch where it caches its food and steal it for themselves, and then go on to hunt and eat the fox.[21] The Eskimos in particular have traditionally hunted Arctic foxes by tying a sharpened piece of whalebone into a bow-shaped spring with a thong, then covering the spring with fat and leaving it to freeze. When the fat hardens, the thong is cut, and the concealed spring is left out as bait for foxes, which are killed when the fat thaws in their stomach

and the whalebone springs open to pierce their internal organs.[22]

Arctic foxes became an unexpected source of food for European explorers of the Arctic, who started off projecting onto the white fox the disgust they held for the familiar red fox. Captain George Lyon reported that on one long expedition his men were all 'horrified at the idea of eating foxes, but very many soon got the better of their delicacy and found them good eating. Not being very nice myself, I soon made the experiment, and found the flesh much resembling that of kid, and afterward frequently had a supper of it.'[23] Lyon's report resembles that of many explorers who, upon need, overcome their revulsion at the idea of eating an animal that lies outside their customary diet and then find that it actually resembles another animal lying within the accepted bounds of edibility.

An Arctic fox at sunset. The Arctic fox is one of the few species that humans consider edible.

143

In South America the *culpeo* and *chilla* were hunted around Lake Titicaca by the Inca, although they were probably eaten only by the lower classes, and disdained by royalty.[24] Further north, in Mexico, the Aztecs kept zoos in which were found what were probably grey foxes. The Spanish conquistador Hernando Cortez described how Montezuma had a large and beautiful house filled with birds of prey, lions, wolves and foxes that were fed poultry as well as the flesh of human sacrificial victims.[25] It is probable that these zoos were not the repositories of human food, but, as zoos are today, collections whose variety and sheer numbers were intended to display a mastery over nature by which even undomesticated animals were made dependent on humans. In that sense, the Aztec foxes would count more as pets than as food, but the two categories are often close, since the acquisition of animals for display or for consumption as food has the same result of making them into commodities.

During the dynasties of the Old Kingdom of Egypt (2700–2159 BC), attempts were made to domesticate the fox in order to keep it as a regular source of food.[26] Almost certainly the fox known to the Egyptians would have been the fennec, which is common to northern parts of the African continent, is unscented, and is especially known to make a delightful pet. Even today fennecs continue to be eaten throughout the Sahara, as reported by Knut Schmidt-Nielson: 'young fennecs are born in the burrow in the early spring, and the Arabs frequently dig them out and sell them to the settled population in the oases, where they are fattened to be eaten when they grow up'.[27] Now, Schmidt-Nielson has more interest in animal behaviour than in what humans eat or in the marketing of wild animals as pets, but, like most commentators on the fennec, he drops his dispassionate scientific façade with the admission that his study took on a closer and more personal quality: 'I had two of these delightful animals as

A fox chained to a car in rural Minnesota, 1940. Most attempts to make foxes into pets end in frustration.

house pets in the Sahara, and later was able to have them in my home in the United States.'[28] Schmidt-Nielson would certainly claim that he kept his fennecs for scientific observation rather than as companions. But either way, by observing their behaviour or delighting in their antics, he has become kind of consumer, cultivating them just as the Arabs do who fatten them up for what is simply a more physical consumption.

Fennecs have attracted so many exotic pet fanciers that a young breeding pair can fetch $1,500 in America. But advertisements for pet fennecs carry an important warning to pet lovers that yearn, like Schmidt-Nielson, to bring some of these adorable little foxes into their homes. Fennecs are listed on CITES Appendix II, which is the posting by the Convention on International Trade in Endangered Species of animals that have become threatened by trade or destruction of habitat and cannot be traded across national boundaries.

The fawning descriptions of fennecs by field zoologists puts this species of fox into a distinct category. Red foxes are seldom described as charming or delightful, and almost never appear as pets. David Macdonald has raised numerous foxes in his home, though not with the intention of keeping them as pets. In his book *Running With the Fox*, one of his side bars is titled 'Are Foxes Good Pets?', a question he answers in the negative. He points to the tendency of older cubs to chew up leather in all forms, as well as electrical wiring; and then, as he says, 'I have always rather liked the lingering smell of fox urine, but it is noteworthy that one landlady was unable to find another tenant for several months after my fox and I vacated the property.'[29]

The smell that accompanies many species probably contributes to the visceral reaction that most people have to the fox, which keeps it from finding a place in the list of desirable pets. But most of all there is the traditional belief that a fox simply cannot be trusted. E. T. Seton states very plainly that though the grey fox has no smell 'as a pet, however, we have not found him particularly interesting . . . and we have never seen one that was more than half tame'.[30]

As un-domesticable animals, as dubious pets, foxes will always be outside human culture – they remain outlaws, embodiments of what humans, with our need to form regulated groups, cannot abide or understand. Louise Robbins points out that, when people began to keep exotic pets in the eighteenth century, the species most commonly sought out were ones like monkeys and parrots that seemed to mimic human gestures and speech.[31] Foxes do not reflect an image of ourselves: their vertically slit pupils, their smell and their solitary, elusive nature keep them well beyond the reach of our affection.

The trouble posed by fox pets reflects much of the way that humans in the West and in Asia have long thought of foxes generally as untrustworthy, wicked and possessed of illegitimate powers. Foxes may be exploited for sport, but only by upholding the myth that they pose a threat. They can even be cultivated – in factory-like conditions of mind-numbing brutality – for their pelts, and with such success that their fur loses all distinction and is sold as fake fur. With that development the fox has evaded domestication again: since the fur taken from foxes is sold as fake, it is voided of the distinct value that would give it a place in the capitalist

A three-year-old dog fox in safe hands. From a 1930s book on fox-hunting.

economy. Voided of the power it once held for the Lindow Man, fox fur in its modern commercial form is disguised beyond all recognition, even to the point where its connection with an animal is denied. It no longer embodies primordial power or barbaric opulence, but is said to be ersatz. In the extremity of its exploitation of animals and their mythic powers, the fur industry shows more plainly than perhaps any other capitalist enterprise that to find a use-value for something inherently wild, an animal that will never form a productive part of the barnyard menagerie, can result only in divorcing it from its actual being and even from the value it has accrued through cultural histories.

6 Twentieth-century Fox: The Cinema

The different characters given to foxes by different cultures determine the roles they play in national cinemas. Because film is such a modern medium, cinematic characters reflect twenti-eth- and twenty-first-century interpretations of cultural themes and events more than they do earlier interpretive myths. The character of Reynard, for example, certainly reappears in fox films, but not necessarily in the context of the beast epic that made the medieval characterization satirical. Correspondingly, the Asian spirit-fox does not always come to the screen in a direct rehearsal of the literary narratives, but in a roundabout or – appropriately for a fox – subterranean manner.

Cinematic foxes most often appear in allegorical form, with the notable exception of *The Belstone Fox* (1973), in which an un-catchable fox leads the local pack on some legendary chases. Tag, the fox, grows up with a foxhound, Merlin, and together they turn the serious business of fox-hunting into a game, per-petuating the traditional myth that foxes enjoy the hunt. But, of course, friendly relations between species that are supposed to be at war violate natural alignments so that the huntsman who had sanctioned the friendship meets a tragic end. But for the most part, the foxes appearing on screen are fox in name only, relying on the tradition that has lent particular attributes to them, as in *The Grey Fox* (1982), where Richard Farnsworth plays

James Hill's *The Belstone Fox* (1973). The foxhound licking the fox in the lap of the MFH's daughter. When a loyal hound befriends an outlaw, the fun turns to anguish.

an old train robber who had once been ingenious as a thief (or any of the countless TV and film versions of *Zorro* – whose name is simply the Spanish word for 'fox'). What matters in these presentations, which are very general, is the way in which popular culture reveals its view of what a fox stands for – that is, what qualities can be signified through references to the fox – for cinema reflects the broad assumptions of society and necessarily anthropomorphizes natural beings like the fox. Along with the linguistic uses of 'fox', cinematic portrayals of foxes reveal the complex and often contradictory attitudes that human beings hold towards them.

As a particularly modern cultural form, films deserve special consideration because they reflect the ways in which Reynard and the spirit-fox tales have been reinterpreted after the heyday of fox-hunting and after the entry of China, Korea and Japan into the capitalist free market, where elements of a cultural past become commodities. For the first time foxes appear as predators and conniving seducers and thieves only seldom, instead turning up as victims. Even when they do steal, as in the case of Bill Miner the Grey Fox, it is because they are outcasts driven by a longing that cannot belong to the mainstream bourgeois world. What remains from the mythic systems is the association of the fox with a subterranean power that is often cast as sexuality, since – especially in the West – that is the force on which fears and anxieties are most focused, with the result that sex is made to seem wicked or uncontrollable.

In the Looney Tunes cartoon of 1939, *Robin Hood Makes Good*, three young squirrels have been reading the tales of Robin Hood and decide to play at being the famous thief of Sherwood Forest. A hungry fox spying on the squirrels recognizes their game as an opportunity to draw them into his clutches. Fundamentally, this story re-enacts Reynard's seduction of the geese, except that instead of playing the role of preacher or mendicant in order to lure the naive geese, this cartoon fox pretends to be Maid Marion in distress. But just as the medieval geese are very often feminine in order to suggest that Reynard's hunger represents all worldly lust, the twentieth-century squirrels are very like children lusted after by a sexual predator. The Looney Tunes fox leers at the tender young rodents, and he salivates over their gambols and larks. But when he is tricked in his turn by the youngest and smallest of the squirrels into believing

The fox as sexual predator is undone by the innocence of squirrels in Chuck Jones's *Robin Hood Makes Good* (1939).

that the local hunt has struck his trail, he literally turns yellow – indicating that he has lost the fire of his lust – and flees. Innocence is restored, and vulpine predation – and sexuality – are revealed as illegitimate and unsustainable.

The connection of the cartoon fox to sexual fire reappears in the characterization of foxes by Michael Powell, Alfred Hitchcock, Mark Rydell and Rainer Werner Fassbinder, as well as Asian directors such as Stanley Tong and Kim Hyeong-Il. Powell's film of 1950, *Gone to Earth*, gives the most prominent role to any non-allegorical fox outside documentary or cartoons, but even this one expands from the literal presentation to a broader allegory involving humans as foxes. The young vixen, Foxy, adopted as more than a pet by Hazel Woodus, provides the focus for the triangular conflict between Hazel, Jack Reddin – the local fox-hunting squire – and Edward Marston, the Low-Church minister.

For gentle Edward, Hazel's relations with Foxy is part of the naturalness that makes her attractive. In marrying her he hopes to protect her and her pets from predators like Reddin, of whom Hazel says: 'he's got the blood of little foxes on him'. The first time Hazel goes to Reddin's house, one of the foxhounds

Michael Powell and Emeric Pressburger's *Gone to Earth* (1950). The gentle minister caresses Foxy, believing that Hazel is too fragile for sex.

Gone to Earth. Defying the social restrictions against foxes, Hazel insists that her closest friend takes part in her wedding with Edward.

growls ominously at her, leading her to tell the squire that she 'canna-d-abear the hound dogs . . . They kills the poor foxes'.[1] The polar opposite of Edward, Reddin chases Hazel aggressively, allegorically turning her into the fox of his sexual hunt.

Hazel herself personifies the fox in a complex series of identifications that turn the simple story of sexual predation into a rich account of social – and species – alignments. Hazel repeatedly refers to herself as 'Foxy's mam', and her own mother was a Gypsy who left the girl a book of magic spells and charms. These spells all revolve around local landmarks that, as Mary Webb puts it in the novel, are 'cowled in ancient legends', pointing to a primordial power available to those who live close to the earth.[2] Hazel is indeed so close to the earth that it is the foxfire in her that makes her mother's spells work for her, and enables her to commune with the animals, and makes her attractive to both Reddin and Edward. But as the Gypsy daughter who has inherited this strange power, Hazel, like the fox, is cast out from a society that can see her power only in sexual terms. Her Aunt Prowde expels her from the house out of fear that she will attract cousin Albert. Similarly, when Edward falls in love with the Gypsy girl, the elder Mrs Marston warns him off, saying: 'Whether it is mistaken kindness, or a silly flirtation, it will only do you harm.'[3]

Edward considers Hazel to be a creature of nature too fragile to have sex with, as she incites a desire in him that his Low-Church morality has not equipped him to act upon. Edward cannot help but recognize how beautiful Hazel is, but he responds by trying to preserve her supposed natural state from predatory exploitation. In a touching scene, complicated by the fact that Hazel has become intrigued by the sporting squire's persistent sexual advances, Edward quietly expresses interest in the Gypsy mother's charms, unaware that these will compel his wife to go to Reddin. Hazel, played by the sultry Jennifer Jones, wants what Edward is afraid to give her, sex, and like everything else about her her desire for sex comes from the earth. When Hazel performs the 'Harper Charm' from the book of spells to learn how to respond to Reddin, she hears the fate she had hoped for, and says to Foxy 'I'm bound to go'.[4] She is indeed bound, by the charm, by the mountain and by the heritage of her mother – that is to say, she is bound by the earth itself that compels her sexually towards the man who will destroy her and

Hazel and Foxy are titillated by the sound of the foxhunting squire's 'Holloa' in *Gone to Earth*.

away from the man who would protect her but who does not satisfy her fiery and chthonic sexual desire.

The sexual hunting metaphor complete, or rather consummated, Hazel attempts to escape from Reddin's trap. In the final sequence, the squire serves as hunt master leading the field after their prey, which turns out to be Foxy. Hazel tries to carry her dearest friend to safety – to Edward's parsonage – but just as the foxhounds are about to drag the two of them down, she falls into an abandoned mine shaft, and is literally gone to earth. The particular form of her death tells us in no uncertain terms how much she has been victimized through her innocence. But the death is also her return to her proper place, the earth from which her fiery beauty emanated, and which had bound her to go to her destroyer.

The contrast between Jack Reddin and Edward Marston parallels that between the fox-hunting establishment and animal rights activists, each promoting a different limited understanding of the earth and of the fox, each believing firmly that theirs is the true version of nature. For Edward, nature – found in Hazel, Foxy and the Gypsy lore – should be protected, as the weak are protected by the strong and just. For Reddin, nature exists to give itself up to human cultivation. Hazel feels mostly ill at ease in Edward's house – dominated as it is by the minister's mother, who thinks it 'a pity' that Hazel should look so wild.[5] In Reddin's house Hazel lounges about in post-coital ease. The novel says that Hazel 'was fascinated by Reddin; she was drawn to confide in Edward; but she wanted neither of them', for her passion cannot be fully comprehended in either Reddin's predatory terms or Edward's protective ones.[6]

As embodiment of the callous upper-class domination of the landscape, Powell's Jack Reddin illustrates how far fox-hunting had declined as a social institution by the mid-twentieth century.

Alfred Hitchcock's *Marnie* (1964). Marnie tries to placate her mother with a fox-fur neckpiece.

Alfred Hitchcock's *Marnie* (1964) also employs the hunt as an emblem of an aristocracy that exploits sexual victims, in this case through repression. The psychoanalytic trappings of the film never reach beyond flummery, but in framing the plot they emphasize the effect of interdicting the kill of the fox-hunt by connecting it to the unnameable sexual act. Appropriately for a psychologically laden film, the fox, with its sexual associations, has been sublimated into aristocratic refinement and is never visible, though it lies just outside the frame, always on the verge of making the appearance that would disrupt the smooth social order of Virginia's fox-hunting aristocracy.

The title character, Marnie, played by Tippie Hedren, has concealed her sordid childhood in the Baltimore docks by adopting a polished finishing-school accent and learning to type, in order to use her charm and looks to get strategically placed secretarial positions and embezzle substantial sums of money to support her love of horses. With her pouting lower lip and her passion for big thoroughbreds, Marnie is almost as sexually alluring as Hazel Woodus; but Marnie's is Virginian sexuality, repressed and utterly without Hazel's frankness.

The repressed Marnie panics during a Virginia hunt.

When Marnie gets a position in the firm of Mark Rutland, scion of an old Virginia fox-hunting family, she charms him into overlooking her panic attacks brought on whenever she sees the colour red, with the result that he falls, somewhat inexplicably, in love with her. When she pilfers his company safe, Mark finds her at The Red Fox Inn, and uses his knowledge of her criminal behaviour to blackmail her into marrying him. The problem is that Marnie is mysteriously repelled by the prospect of any sexual contact, and so their marriage can never be consummated.

Nonetheless, the married couple fits in almost seamlessly into the family life on the Rutland estate, which is dominated by sexual tensions whose only outlet is the fox-hunt. All this repressed Virginian sexuality explodes on the hunt when Marnie, properly looking away from the fox to the huntsman's scarlet coat, is seized with panic and gallops off, coming out of her attack just as her horse falls and breaks its neck. When Mark's jealous sister, Lil, offers to shoot the suffering animal, Marnie sneers: 'Haven't you had enough killing?' The reference is both to the institutional hunt embraced by the Virginia society in which the Rutlands play a prominent role and to Marnie's own repressed past.

Through a few more scenes, and a bit more psychoanalytic flummery, we learn that Marnie's mother had been a prostitute who made her daughter sleep on the sofa whenever a man called. One night, during a thunderstorm, a sailor left the bedroom when he heard Marnie crying and tried to comfort her; the mother sought to protect her daughter from contact with a sex-customer, and Marnie cracked his head open with a poker, causing blood to stain his white uniform – hence her terror concerning the colour red, and her revulsion for physical contact with men.

Even as a thief and a liar, Marnie is the victim of the code that suppresses open talk of sex and death. Without showing a single real fox, the film allegorically portrays the one who repeatedly challenges men to chase her, and *Marnie* thereby makes vulpine victimization the hinge of institutional repression of sex and desire. The hunt scene compels Marnie to confront her complicity in the repressive social institution and the fact that she embodies what must be repressed. This explosive confrontation allows her to open herself to her past of poverty,

The red effect begins . . .

violence and sex (along with thunder and the colour red), and to heal sufficiently that she will almost certainly soon enjoy conjugal relations with her husband.

If all this seems a bit overwrought, well, it is worth remembering that *Marnie* has never stood out as one of Hitchcock's more successful ventures, and, in fact, the legend surrounding the film is that Hitchcock lost interest in the project when Hedren rebuffed his sexual advances. But for all its flaws, the film relies on the traditional characterization of the fox, and the strategic interdiction at the heart of institutionalized fox-hunting to give substance to the psychoanalytic frame of sexual repression.

Mark Rydell's *The Fox* (1968), based on D. H. Lawrence's novella of the same name, maintains the direct association of the fox with sex along with the prohibition of speaking openly about sexual desire. Of the two women living together, trying to make a go of farming, March (Anne Heywood) frankly acknowledges to herself that she wants sex, while Jill (Sandy Denis) is so repressed that she fails to understand her friend's need, or even her own. A fox meanwhile has been stealing the chickens that

On his way to the henhouse, the fox in Mark Rydell's film (1968) watches March (Anne Heywood) fantasizing in the woods.

Jill loves and coddles (an extreme version of Edward Marston's protective sympathy for Hazel and Foxy), so March ventures out to shoot the predator. Standing alone in the forest, March begins to indulge the masturbatory fantasies that fill her nights, when she notices that the fox is watching her. She does not shoot the fox, but only stares back, telling Jill afterwards that the encounter was 'odd' and 'strange', as though it held portentous significance. Later, when Paul intrudes into the household, captivating March as the fox had done – and satisfying her sexual longing – Jill is at first oblivious to the sexual energy generated by his presence and then increasingly hostile as she finally has to recognize March's sexual desire for Paul. Jill's interest in a sexual triangle (or in any form of sex) does not include the act itself, and March begins to feel pressurized into renouncing her relations with Paul and resuming the repressed arrangement with Jill. Paul has something of the predator in him, and one night, after hearing March comfort Jill with the promise that he will be gone soon, he shoots the fox, nailing its carcass to the barn door. With this act Paul establishes himself as the official lover of March, and urges her to move towards sexual respectability by marrying him. Their marriage would exclude Jill, however, and much of the last third of the story concerns the conflict that March feels over loyalty to her friend and their unorthodox arrangement (which had hovered on the verge of developing into a sexual relationship) and the physical satisfaction she has found with Paul. When Jill dies through what might be a self-sacrifice, March leaves the farm with Paul, apparently aware that the conventional relationship she will have with him will curtail the freedom of self-determination she had with Jill. The film closes with a shot of the fox nailed to the barn door, decayed and rain-soaked, suggesting that the passion and beauty – even frustrated as it was – had been available

Paul becomes the predatory fox as sexual tensions mount by the barn in *The Fox*.

to March only until she took up her conventional relationship with Paul.

Like *Gone to Earth* and *Marnie*, Rydell's film makes the fox into an emblem of a complicated sexual energy that cannot be confined to the conventional heterosexual partnership of marriage. The weakness of the film is that it depends on D. H. Lawrence's own limited view of any unconventional sexual expression (the lesbianism that never quite happens); but its strength is that it likewise explores the problems attendant on not bringing sexual energy to full expression. Considered within the context of other fox films, Rydell's vulpine sexuality gestures towards a recognition that the subterranean power of the fox – the primordial foxfire – may find partial expression in sex, but still exceeds even that. The fear and anxiety that in British and American society accompany sex beyond its confinement in conventional marriage make the association of more widely ranging sexuality with the fox almost unavoidable, considering the long tradition associating foxes with wickedness, elusiveness and chthonic forces. The ending of *The Fox* suggests that March will almost certainly not remain satisfied with Paul, that her sexual needs extend beyond what he can understand. Their relationship is bound to entail the same unnameable frustration that had loomed large in that between March and Jill. The frustration is unspeakable because March's sexual longing exceeds both relationships; neither has the language to enable March to express the energy of her desire, and the inevitable result is that the desire continues to appear unconventional at best and illegitimate at worst. This is the same kind of interdiction that governs the Virginia hunting society in *Marnie*, and that is illustrated in the contrast between Edward Marston and Jack Reddin.

The connections between foxes and sexual desire are explored further, and in a somewhat different direction, by the German director Rainer Werner Fassbinder through images and motifs from the medieval Reynard tradition recast in the context of post-Second World War politics. Early in his too-brief career, Fassbinder identified himself as a fox by playing the lead role in his film *Fox and his Friends* (1975). To make the identification as plain as possible, the Fassbinder character wears his name, 'Fox', in silver studs on the back of his coat. The story

Fox wearing his coat in Rainer Werner Fassbinder's *Fox and his Friends* (1975).

is of a working-class homosexual man who steals the price of what proves to be a winning lottery ticket. Fox's 'friends' flock around him, attracted by his new wealth, and peck him clean. The unsuspecting Fox is taken in by Eugen, whose family business has suffered some financial strain, and whose bourgeois distaste for the working class makes his interest in Fox suspicious. Eugen's fashionable homosexual friends deride Fox openly, calling him a monster and complaining about his smell – both the literal one emanating from his dirty socks and the metaphorical one surrounding his proletarian manners. The desperate love that Fox feels for Eugen reflects the working-class desire to move up into the bourgeoisie, buttressed by the belief that the money from his lottery winnings can buy him legitimacy. In the end, after Eugen swindles him out of the lottery money, Fox commits suicide. The final scene shows Fox lying dead while two other gay men carelessly plan a holiday romp and a pair of schoolboys pick through the dead Fox's pockets.

Fox and his Friends frames its plot through allegorical references to *Reineke Fuchs*. The final scene provides a straightforward depiction of the dead fox surrounded by ravens, a common motif in church carvings throughout Europe. Fox's bad odour and proletarian manners repel the bourgeois Eugen, making him uncomfortably aware of the tawdriness of his circle of friends, who pick up young men in public toilet. Fox is made susceptible by his desire both for Eugen and for a place in the bourgeoisie who exploit and destroy him. It is desire, which may be interpreted as either lust or longing, that makes Fox vulnerable to the ravens that are always waiting to swarm on him.

In ways that are too complex to describe here, Fassbinder continued throughout his career to use vulpine motifs to portray the forbidden desire and longings that threaten to destroy people – and nations. (The last of the BDR Trilogy, *The Longing of Veronika Voss*, alludes to the old Low German word for fox, *Vos*, in a tangled alignment of drug addiction, vulpitude and Germany's Nazi past.) Desire compels the fox to commit most of his crimes, as illustrated in the carving in Ely Cathedral of Reynard saying to the flock of geese: '*Testis est mihi Deus quam cupian vos omnes visceribus meus*' ('God is my witness how I long for you in my bowels'). Reynard is driven wholly by desire, which manifests itself as simple lust as well as the more ineffable sense of longing, as Fassbinder shows throughout these films. Longing plays a much more obvious role in the Asian foxes, however.

Given the wide range of tales in China, Korea and Japan about spirit foxes, Asian cinema has a wealth of fox lore to exploit. Beginning in the 1990s, Hong Kong studios combined the martial arts formula with adaptations of the seventeenth-century tales of spirit-foxes collected by Pu Songling to create rich fantasies about romantic love between humans and spirits. The *Fox Ghost* of 2002, directed by Stanley Tong, stands out among Hong Kong films as the most overt presentation of the sexual element of the spirit-fox tradition, combining several of Pu's fox narratives to tell of a student, Tao Wang San, who becomes entangled with spirit-foxes when he marries the beautiful Xiao-you and lives on her estate, which is haunted by foxes. On the wedding night, after watching husband and wife repeatedly consummate their marriage vows, the female spirit-foxes decide that they would like to experience the same degree of pleasure and satisfaction, but are unable to discover the proper technique, despite a great deal of fondling and cuddling. Their desire increases as they follow Tao and Xiao-you's lovemaking in the woods, by the river, and at breakfast, lunch and dinner. Aware that his lovemaking has been watched, Tao attempts to placate the spirit-foxes, hoping they will leave, but they only

Tao frightens his brothers with a fox carcass in Stanley Tong's *Fox Ghost* (2002).

You're so timid. It's just a toy
Give me some tea

condemn his prayers. When he then offers them the same satisfaction he has given Xiao-you, however, the worlds of spirit-foxes and human mortals become united in beautiful harmony – and three-way sex.

Rainia Huntington points out in her study of spirit-fox narratives that 'sex is one of the possible aspects of an exchange with the spirit world', although it is not the only one.[7] She points to a traditional analogy, that the most lustful people are prostitutes, just as the most lustful animals are foxes, to emphasize the point that sex with spirit-foxes seldom brings enlightenment but only bewitchment. Foxes, Huntington stresses, represent the sexual depletion that seems both frightening and alien to men, which explains why later tales cast foxes increasingly as mere sexual vampires.[8]

The vampire element – though without its sexual element – achieved its fullest development in 2004, when Korean television, KBS, aired Kim Hyeong-il's *Gumiho*, or *The Nine-Tailed Fox*, about a secret race of spirit-foxes living in modern society, intermixing with humans who are mostly unaware of their existence. The human ignorance is understandable, since these foxes look just like ordinary people – except more eye-catching. But that

Si yon admits to the man she loves that she is also an assassin for the nine-tailed foxes. From Kim Hyeong-il's *Gumiho* (2004).

Yes, it's true...
I'm a nine-tailed fox.

ignorance also follows from the setting of the series in twenty-first-century urban Korea, which, in looking to the West for its popular consumer culture, has forgotten its own cultural legends. Following the lines of traditional Asian fox narratives, there is the impossible love of a fox-woman, Si yon (Kim Tae Hee), for a human man (indeed, the alternate English title is *Forbidden Love*), but this time she happens to be a warrior trained from youth to defend the elder nine-tailed foxes, and to kill humans without mercy. The man she loves, Min woo (Jo Hyeon-Jae), happens to be a detective in the ultra-secret Special Investigative Corporation Services, or SICS, organized solely to hunt down and destroy the race of nine-tailed foxes. But he also happens to be Si yon's childhood friend whom she thought murdered by the band of marauding spirit-foxes who killed her parents and his during a birthday celebration for the two children, who happened to be born on the same day.

The facts that Min woo and Si yon have the same birthday, that they were violently separated when they were both exactly twelve years old, and that he is a human and she a fox all become fraught with meaning as the plot unfolds over sixteen episodes. In the legend as it is presented in this series, foxes once ruled the world but were overthrown by humans and have had to live in secrecy ever since. Nine-tailed foxes, or in Korean, *gumiho*, are those foxes that have attained enlightenment sufficient to shape-shift into humans (their nine tails indicate their advanced development). In this show they continue to be the superior race, though seriously flawed by their vampiric need to eat human liver in order to survive. Once a millennium a thousand-year-old fox is born into the race of nine-tailed foxes that alone holds the possibility of ending the foxes' curse of having to prey on the human organ and thereby making it possible for foxes and humans to live together in peace. That possibility, highly desired by the foxes, can be realized only if the thousand-year-old fox remains a virgin and is sacrificed by the chief elder fox on the night of the red moon eclipse – which also happens only in a millennium. Earlier chances were all foiled when the thousand-year-old fox fell in love with a human.

Unlike the Hong Kong presentations of Pu Songling's stories, *The Nine-Tailed Fox* is set as a contemporary narrative in modern bourgeois Korea. Although the foxes drive big American cars, listen to rap music and sport black leather outfits, it is they, not the humans, who hold on to indigenous Korean culture, albeit with a secrecy as strict as that guarding their vulpine nature. Their secret temple lies hidden underground, beneath the natural history museum, where the chief elder is head anthropologist. The walls of this temple are covered with carvings of nine-tailed foxes, and serve as the repository for the ancient lore that guides the fox race in their struggle to survive in the modern age and in their hope to regain their former prominence.

The humans, on the other hand, present a deracinated Korean culture that has become so westernized as to regard its indigenous legends as nonsense. 'A race of liver-eating foxes – does that make sense to you?' is how Min woo's partner, Detective Moon, responds to the explanation for the necessity of the sics. Repeatedly, throughout the sixteen episodes, the conflict between foxes and sics is cast as that between two races – the one seeking to live in harmony, the other trying only to destroy the first. In the penultimate episode, in which Si yon comes to accept her destiny as the thousand-year-old fox and decides to sacrifice herself so that the two races can live together, she asks Min woo (who wants her to elope with him and who knows only that she is a nine-tailed fox but not that she is the thousand-year-old fox) to resist making any move against the foxes until after the full moon. She cannot tell him that she plans to sacrifice herself, saying only that she must do something for her race. He explodes in anger, sneering at her: 'that's what it's all about, being a nine-tailed fox. Just as you have something to do for your race, so I have something to do for mine.' And what he means – the secret he is keeping from her – is that he has acquired the single weapon that can destroy the fox clan, the Red Moon sword, and he intends to use it.

The implication of Min woo's murderous plan is that the westernized modern Korean must turn away from its indigenous culture of legends and traditions and embrace a European understanding of what it means to be human. Correspondingly, the implication of Si yon's decision to sacrifice herself is that a great force continues to exist in Korea that is more powerful and older than anything offered by the West. The *gumiho* constitutes the primordial chthonic force that is on the verge of being annihilated once and for all. Like the Greek Teumessian fox, from which Thebes sought to liberate itself in order to enter the modern world, the *gumiho* threatens to prevent Korea from redefining itself in modern Western terms. But the bittersweet fact that Si yon succeeds in sacrificing herself provides the possibility that both the indigenous and the new cultures can coexist, the one infusing a native power into the other.

If *Gumiho* is seductive in its visual appeal, it is haunting in its political implication; and that is how a fox film should be, for foxes are themselves ambivalently appealing and troubling, having never been domesticated. Foxes make bad pets because they are supposed to be thieves and seducers. From the vertically slit pupils of their eyes, to their colour and the shape of their tail, to their subterranean habitations, foxes have long represented a kind of life that human cultures around the world have worked hard to hold at bay. Aristotle says that the fox is wicked because its earthiness calls to mind those chthonic powers that human culture attempts to rise above. Modern scientific names for different fox genera and species repeat Aristotle's condemnation because foxes wickedly confuse and disrupt attempts at a coherent taxonomy. The moral judgement reaches its pinnacle in the institution of English foxhunting, which ritualistically re-enacts the trial and execution of

As responsible parents, foxes teach their children to be thieves and outlaws from an early age.

168

An Arctic fox in summer coloration enjoys Alaskan poppies.

Reynard the thief in a way that makes culture safe, whole and clean. But the ubiquity of fox fur, especially as it has come to be disguised as unreal fur, reminds us that, however we condemn them, torment them, trap them and exploit them, foxes live close to human culture by defining the limits of that culture. The vulpine characters of cinema complicate these limits by illustrating that the expulsion of chthonic vulpine energy amounts to little more than a brand of sexual repression and cultural deracination. Fox narratives from the Theban myth of the Teumessian vixen to *Gumiho* strongly suggest that we humans have always been uncomfortable in recognizing a bit too much of ourselves in the fox – and too much of the fox in ourselves – and that we therefore assert our distinctive humanness by interdicting, suppressing and forgetting our own vulpitude.

Timeline of the Fox

55 million BC	3.5 million BC	3 million BC	1.25 million BC
Vulpids begin to appear in forms distinct from other canids, retaining enough non-canid qualities to make them seem ambiguously like cats	Ancestors of the grey fox appear in North America, while the *culpeo* – typical of South American foxes in being unrelated to any other fox species – spreads throughout the pampas	*Vulpes alepecoides,* ancestor of both red and Arctic foxes, appears	Red fox ancestors migrate northern Europe, becomi extinct in their original North American range

600 BC	4th century BC	c. 300 BC–AD 1650	c. AD 900
Aesop aligns the fox with the illegitimate and frightening form of intelligence, *metis*, contributing to the Western view that the fox is evil	Aristotle provides a scientific basis for the Western bias against the fox when he condemns it for eluding empirical investigation	Throughout Europe large groups of red foxes are burnt alive in ritual immolations aimed at harnessing the animal's elusive and fiery power	In China gentlemen begin relating tales of spirit-foxes seducing humans, while in Europe Reynard's various crimes begin to be depicted in churches

1869	1845	1914
Two prominent British actresses are portrayed in glamorous attire trimmed in fox fur, denoting the start of a widespread desire to raise foxes within a controlled environment exclusively for the sake of their fur	Red foxes are introduced into Australia by sportsmen wishing to emulate the great English chases made famous by sports journalists like 'Nimrod' 	Siegfried Sassoon forsakes the comfortable life of a gentleman hunting foxes in England to kill Germans in the trenches of France. In *Memoirs of a Foxhunting Man* he explains how the war made it impossible for him to return to fox-hunting

1 million BC	300,000 BC	100,000 BC	650 BC
The corsac, a *Vulpes* species, appears on the Asian steppe in a form close to its current shape	The modern *Vulpes* species migrates back to North America, evolving into the kit foxes and swift foxes prevalent throughout the western half of the continent until the major glaciers recede	With glaciers covering most of Europe and Asia, the range of the modern Arctic fox extends from southern France to Siberia	A giant vixen, lurking outside the city of Thebes, plagues the citizens by eating their children; she provides the archetype for the evil force destroyed by the newly arrived saviour, in this case either Amphitryon or Oedipus

c. 1100–1140	c. 1550	1661	1750
The Japanese artist Toba Sojo depicts spirit-foxes igniting their tails in order to transform themselves into human form	Young Incan men assume the identity of the fox in the family of animals in order to qualify as guardian in the family of humans	Samuel Pepys employs a full range of vulpine terms in reference to the gentle art of bibulism	Hugo Meynell becomes master of the Quorn Hunt and perfects the modern form of fox-hunting; within a century the fox is declared one of the three most important animals in England, along with the foxhound and the thoroughbred horse

1950	2004	2005
Michael Powell brings Mary Webb's novel *Gone to Earth* to the screen, using Jennifer Jones's sultry character both to reaffirm the chthonic sexuality of foxes and to attack the fox-hunting institution as a wanton exploiter of nature for selfish ends	The Korean television network KBS broadcasts the series *Gumiho*, revealing the existence of a race of spirit-foxes that has infiltrated human society 	The British Parliament bans hunting foxes with packs of hounds

Evolution Charts

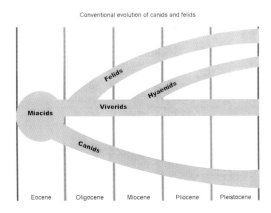

Conventional evolution of canids and felids

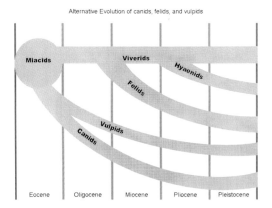

Alternative Evolution of canids, felids, and vulpids

The top chart illustrates the conventional view that all canids evolved in a fundamentally different direction from cats. The second chart presents an alternative view: that vulpids broke off from other animals early enough to retain cat-like features.

Genera and Species of Fox Worldwide

GENUS *ALOPEX*

Alopex lagopus, Arctic fox, is the single species in this genus, though there are two colour morphs, one white in winter, grey to dark brown in summer, the other grey to black (known as 'blue phase') with little seasonal change. Inhabits the Arctic region wherever the red fox is absent. Body 53 cm, tail 30 cm. Omniverous, nocturnal. Migrates more than 1,000 km. During the mating season one male groups with two females, otherwise solitary.

GENUS *ATELOCYNUS*

Atelocynus microtis, Small-eared fox, is the single species. Found from the Amazon north throughout Panama in tropical jungle. Body 85 cm, tail 30 cm. Dark brown to grey. Almost nothing is known of natural habits. Of a pair in Chicago Zoo, the male was friendly, the female growled at humans. The taxonomy of this animal is in dispute, with some naturalists denying it is a fox at all.

GENUS *CERDOCYON*

Cerdocyon thous, Crab-eating fox, or Carasissi, is the single species. Inhabits the forested regions of South America. Medium-sized: body 65 cm, tail 30 cm. Brown to grey, round ears. Omniverous, nocturnal. Carasissi are moderately social, grouping in the monogamously mated pair.

GENUS *FENNECUS*

Fennecus zerda, Fennec, is the single species. Inhabits the arid regions of North Africa. Small and cute: body 35 cm, tail 20 cm. Thick fur, tan to light grey. Ears up to 15 cm long. Feet thickly furred. Omniverous and nocturnal. Social and playful; easily tamed. Known to purr.

GENUS *OTOCYON*

Otocyon megalotis, Bat-eared fox is the single species. Lives in arid regions of southern Africa. Medium to small, body 57 cm. Long, rounded ears. Eats insects, vegetation, small vertebrates. Active at all periods. Groups of single male with two females.

GENUS *PSEUDALOPEX*

Pseudalopex culpaeus, Culpeo, is the largest of the genus: body 52–120 cm, tail 30–51 cm. Grey with pale sides and tawny head and neck. Found throughout the semi-arid regions of South America. Eats small vertebrates, eggs, insects, snakes, vegetation. Active at all periods. Little known of social behaviour. Unafraid of humans. Endangered.

Pseudalopex griseus, Chilla. Body 80–90 cm, tail 30–36. Mostly grey; bushy tail has black underside. Lives in Chile and Argentina. Eats rodents, lizards, birds, insects. Active at dawn and dusk. Nothing known of social behaviour except that it is unafraid of humans. Endangered.

Pseudalopex gymnocercus, Pampas fox, or Azara's fox. Body 72 cm, tail 34 cm. Mostly grey with rufous head, black muzzle, white throat; tail tipped black. Found in the eastern parts of South America. Omnivorous and nocturnal. Solitary, pairing only during mating. Unafraid of humans. Endangered.

Pseudalopex sechurae, Sechuran fox. Smallest of the genus. Light grey, with tail tipped black. Inhabits the Sechuran desert of Peru and into the coastal area of Ecuador. Omnivorous and nocturnal. Little is known of this species.

Pseudalopex vetulus, Hoary fox. Body 58–64 cm, tail 28–32 cm. Grey with light underparts, dark tips on ears and tail, short muzzle. Found in parts of central Brazil. Little is known of diet or social behaviour. Active during the day and early evening.

GENUS *UROCYON*

Urocyon cinereoargenteus, Grey fox, Tree fox, Virginia fox, or Colishé. Found throughout wooded areas of United States south of Pennsylvania, Central America, and northern South America. Body 48–73 cm, tail 27–44 cm. Shorter legs than red fox. Mostly grey with bristly dorsal stripe down tail, head is rusty, throat often white, muzzle black and ears ochre. Omnivorous and nocturnal. Nests underground and in trees. Social group consists of mated pair and offspring.

Urocyon littoralis, Island grey fox. Like the grey fox but about 20 per cent smaller, and with two fewer vertebrae in the tail. As with its larger cousin, has long claws for climbing trees. Found on the Channel Islands off the coast of California. Omnivorous and active at all times. Mostly solitary apart from breeding period.

GENUS *VULPES*

Vulpes bengalensis, Bengal fox, or Indian fox. Medium sized, body 50 cm, tail 30 cm. Short fur is buff to silver; tail is not as long as other *Vulpes* species, tipped black. Inhabits the Indian subcontinent, Himalayan foothills, wherever there are open habitats. Omnivorous and nocturnal. Occasionally found in groups. Not wary of humans; easily tamed.

Vulpes cana, Blanford's fox, or Afghan fox. Small, body 40–50 cm, tail 30–41 cm. Dense fur is light to dark grey, with ochre on the legs, and white on the throat. Thought to live from Afghanistan to Iran, and possible in Israel. Mostly eats fruit, but sometimes insects, lizards and rodents. Little is known of its activity.

Vulpes chama, Cape fox. Medium, body 56 cm, tail 33 cm. Short grey fur with black and white mixed throughout, head is dullish red, ears tawny on back and white inside. Found in arid regions of southwest Africa. Nocturnal. Breeds in burrows, and seems to be solitary, though little is known.

Vulpes corsac, the Corsac, or *Kirassu*, is the only species with round pupils. Body 50–60 cm, tail 25–35 cm. Summer fur is grey, winter yellow; the tail tipped brown or black. Slender muzzle and rounded ears. Found throughout Asia in steppes and arid habitats. Wide-ranging diet, mostly nocturnal. Lives in groups, known as corsac cities, hunts in packs. Said by some to be tameable, though this is in dispute.

Vulpes ferrilata, Tibetan sand fox. Body 57–70 cm, tail 40–47 cm. Thick yellow fur. Soles of feet furred. Bushy tail with white-tipped ears. Inhabits the plateaus and high deserts of northern Nepal. Virtually nothing is known of its diet or habits.

Vulpes macrotis, Kit fox, is the smallest of American *Vulpes* species: body 35–50 cm, tail is 40 per cent of body length. Grey to yellow-grey. Large ears. Furred feet. Lives in arid regions of western and central USA and northern Mexico. Carnivorous and nocturnal. Group in mated pairs. Like the fennec, is known to purr.

Vulpes pallida, Pale fox. Medium-sized: body 46 cm, tail 25–35 cm. Pale to buff red. Smaller ears than other desert foxes. Lives in the Sahara. Eats rodents, birds, eggs, reptiles, vegetation. Nocturnal. Burrows communally.

Vulpes rüppelli, Rüppell's fox. Small, body 48–52 cm, tail 25–35 cm. Dense silver fur with dark mark from eyes to upper lip. Large ears. Furred feet. Inhabits the arid regions of north Africa, Arabian peninsula, and western Asia. Omnivorous and nocturnal. Lives in groups of three to five members.

Vulpes velox, Swift fox. Slightly larger than kit foxes; head to tail length is 60–80 cm. Yellow to grey in colour, with black-tipped tail, and dark spot below each eye. Feet furred. Through the plains of central and western North America. Diet varies seasonally. Known to run down jackrabbits. Nocturnal. Grouped in mating pair, sometimes with second female.

Vulpes vulpes, Red fox, is the largest of *Vulpes* species. Body 60–90 cm, tail 30–60 cm. From pale yellowish red to bright orange. 'Silver' foxes are mostly black with silver-tipped guard hairs, and 'cross' foxes have dark dorsal areas and flanks. Limbs are black or dark brown. Found throughout northern hemisphere – largest range of any fox species. Introduced unhappily to Australia. Will eat almost anything. Primarily nocturnal, but active at dusk and dawn. Complex social lives.

References

1 THE FOX IN NATURE

1 Aristotle, *History of Animals*, trans. A. L. Peck (Cambridge, MA, 1965), 487a.
2 Roger French discusses the heat of males and of humans compared to other animals, and the earthiness of bones, in *Ancient Natural History: Histories of Nature* (London, 1994), pp. 59–71.
3 Aristotle, *History of Animals*, 500b.
4 Ibid., 580a.
5 Aristotle, *On Breath*, trans. Walter Stanley Hett (Cambridge, MA, 1975), 477b.
6 Aristotle, *History of Animals*, 589a.
7 Ibid.
8 Plato, *Sophist*, trans. Harold North Fowler (Cambridge, MA, 1987), 239c. Debra Hawhee points out this connection in *Bodily Arts: Rhetoric and Athletics in Ancient Greece* (Austin, TX, 2004), p. 55.
9 Lucretius, *De rerum natura*, trans. Cyril Bailey (Oxford, 1947), V. 857–63.
10 Sappho, *Greek Lyric*, trans. David A. Campbell (Cambridge, MA, 1982), fragment 1. 2.
11 Pliny, *Natural History*, trans. H. Rackham (Cambridge, MA, 1961), p. 423 [X. XCV. 205].
12 For an account of how racial distinctions arose in the eighteenth century, see David Bindman, *Ape to Apollo: Aesthetics and the Idea of Race in the Eighteenth Century* (Ithaca, NY, 2002).
13 George-Louis Leclerc Buffon, *Selections from Natural History, General and Particular*, 4 vols (New York, 1977), vol. IV, pp. 214–15.

14 Ibid., pp. 216 and 197.

15 Ibid., p. 215.

16 Ibid., p. 169.

17 Björn Kurtén and Elain Anderson, *Pleistocene Mammals of North America* (New York, 1980), p. 173.

18 Information on European fossils comes from Björn Kurtén, *Pleistocene Mammals of Europe* (London, 1968), pp. 114–15.

19 Kurtén and Anderson, *Pleistocene Mammals*, p. 174.

20 J. David Henry, *Red Fox: The Catlike Canine* (Washington, DC, 1996), p. 2.

21 Ibid., p. 73. Notably Henry groups the South American foxes into a single genus, *Dusicyon*, which he separates from foxes elsewhere in the world and relates to the dog-like canids.

22 Spencer Fullerton Baird, *Mammals of North America* (Philadelphia, PA, 1857), p. 121.

23 Ernest Thompson Seton, *Lives of Game Animals* (Boston, MA, 1953), vol. I, part 2, p. 578.

24 Jennifer Sheldon, *Wild Dogs: The Natural History of the Nondomestic Canidae* (New York, 1992), p. 125.

25 Charles Darwin, *Voyage of the Beagle* (New York, 1909), p. 297. The taxonomy is debatable. Darwin identifies his fox as *Canis fulvipes*, which many later taxonomists identify as *Dusicyon fulvipes*, although Sheldon says this fox is 'conspecific with *Pseudalopex griseus*' (*Wild Dogs*, p. 5).

26 Sheldon, *Wild Dogs*, p. 63.

27 D. R. Rosevear, *The Carnivores of West Africa* (London, 1974), p. 61.

28 Erik Zimen, 'Introduction: A Short History of Human Attitudes towards the Fox', in *The Red Fox: Symposium on Behaviour and Ecology*, ed. Erik Zimen (The Hague, 1980), p. 1.

29 Huw Glen Lloyd, 'The Red Fox in Britain'; E. D. Ables, 'Ecology of the Red Fox in North America'; both in *The Wild Canids: Their Systematics, Behavioral Ecology and Evolution*, ed. M. W. Fox (New York, 1975), pp. 207 and 234.

30 Zimen, 'Introduction', p. 3.

31 Rebecca Grambo, *The World of the Fox* (San Francisco, 1995), p. 73.

32 Zimen, 'Introduction', p. 4.

33 David Macdonald, *Running with the Fox* (New York, 1987), pp. 56–69.

34 Ibid., p. 12.

35 Ibid., p. 61.

36 Henry, *Red Fox*, p. 71.

37 Von G. Rüppell details the way an adult Arctic fox uses deception in the instruction of her young in 'A "Lie" as a Directed Message of the Arctic Fox (*Alopex lagopus* L.)', in *Deception: Perspectives on Human and Nonhuman Deceit*, ed. Robert W. Mitchell and Nicholas S. Thompson (Albany, NY, 1982), pp. 177–81.

2 VULPINE MYTHS, FOLK TALES AND ALLEGORY

1 Pausanius, *Description of Greece*, trans. W. H. S. Jones (Cambridge, MA, 1918), Boeotia, xix, 1.

2 Apollodorus, *The Library*, trans. Sir James George Frazer (Cambridge, MA, 1921), Bk II. iv. 6–7.

3 *Aesop's Fables*, trans. V. S. Vernon (New York, 1912), p. 203.

4 Ibid., p. 6.

5 *Physiologus*, trans. James Carlill, in *The Epic of the Beast, Consisting of Translations of The History of Reynard the Fox and Physiologus* (London, n. d.), p. 290.

6 Quoted in E. P. Evans, *Animal Symbolism in Ecclesiastical Architecture* (London, 1896), p. 206.

7 Ibid.

8 For a thorough catalogue of ecclesiastical fox carvings in Europe, see Elaine C. Block and Kenneth Varty, 'Choir-Stall Carvings of Reynard and Other Foxes', in *Reynard the Fox: Social Engagement and Cultural Metamorphoses in the Beast Epic from the Middle Ages to the Present*, ed. Kenneth Varty (New York, 2000), pp. 125–62; and see also Kenneth Varty, *Reynard, Renart, Reinaert and Other Foxes in Medieval England: The Iconographic Evidence. A Study of the Illustrating of Fox Lore and Reynard the Fox Stories in England during the Middle Ages* (Amsterdam, 1999). The work of Professor Varty – the undisputed expert on Reynard imagery – has proved

invaluable to my study.

9 Beryl Rowland, *Animals with Human Faces: A Guide to Animal Symbolism* (Knoxville, TN, 1973), p. 76.

10 Donald B. Sands, ed., *The History of Reynard the Fox, Translated and Printed by William Caxton in 1481* (Cambridge, MA, 1960), p. 46.

11 Ibid., p. 55.

12 Ibid., p. 3.

13 Ibid., pp. 77 and 79.

14 R. B. Parker, '*Volpone* and *Reynard the Fox*', *Renaissance Drama*, VII (1977), p. 4.

15 In 1964 Johnny Mercer, Ring Lardner and others collaborated on a musical version of *Volpone*, titled *Foxy*, which played for 72 performances at the Ziegfeld Theatre.

16 Roger Stephenson, 'The Political Import of Goethe's *Reineke Fuchs*', in Varty, ed., *Reynard the Fox*, p. 197.

17 Gary Urton, 'Animal Metaphors and the Life Cycle in an Andean Community', in *Animal Myths and Metaphors in South America*, ed. Gary Urton (Salt Lake City, UT, 1985), p. 255.

18 R. Tom Zuidema, 'The Lion in the City: Royal Symbols of Transition in Cuzco', ibid., p. 187.

19 Urton, 'Animal Metaphors', p. 262.

20 Zuidema, 'The Lion in the City', p. 193.

21 Mircea Eliade, *Shamanism: Archaic Techniques of Ecstasy*, trans. Willard R. Trask (New York, 1964), pp. 90, 102–3.

22 Ralph Merrifield, *The Archaeology of Ritual and Magic* (New York, 1987), p. 32; K. Smith, 'The Excavation of Winklebury Camp, Basingstoke, Hampshire', *Proceedings of the Prehistorical Society*, XLIII (1977), pp. 31–129; Miranda Green, *Animals in Celtic Life and Myth* (London, 1992), p. 125.

23 Anne Ross, 'Lindow Man and the Celtic Tradition', in *Lindow Man: The Body in the Bog*, ed. I. M. Stead, J. B. Bourke and Don Brothwell (London, 1986), pp. 164–6.

24 Sir James Frazer, *The Golden Bough: A Study in Magic and Religion* (New York, 1922), p. 761.

25 Ibid., p. 762.

26 Leo Tak-hung Chan, *The Discourse on Foxes and Ghosts: Ji Yun and Eighteenth-Century Literati Storytelling* (Honolulu, HI, 1998), p. 28.

27 Ibid., pp. 121–2.

28 Ibid., p. 144.

29 Kiyoshi Nozaki, *Kitsunē: Japan's Fox of Mystery, Romance and Humor* (Tokyo, 1961), p. 4.

30 T. Volker, *The Animal in Far Eastern Art, and Especially in the Art of the Japanese Netsuke, with References to Chinese Origins, Traditions, Legends and Art* (Leiden, 1975), p. 76.

31 Michael Bathgate, *The Fox's Craft in Japanese Religion and Folklore: Shapeshifters, Transformations and Duplicities* (New York, 2004), p. 113.

32 I have based this summary on that by Bathgate, *The Fox's Craft*, pp. 3–5. Bathgate adds that 'Tamamo's seduction of Toba was in fact only one episode in a malevolent career that spanned millenia. In ancient India, she had inspired King Hanzoku to invade his neighbors, so that he could perform a grisly sacrificial ritual requiring the heads of one thousand of his fellow kings. In China, she had been the consort of Kin Yu, where her corrupting influence helped to bring about the end of the Western Zhou dynasty' (p. 5).

33 Ibid., p. 7.

34 Chan, *The Discourse on Foxes and Ghosts*, p. 121.

35 Nozaki, *Kitsunē*, pp. 212–13.

36 Carmen Blacker, *The Catalpa Bow: A Study of Shamanistic Practices in Japan* (London, 1975), p. 52.

37 Ibid., pp. 59–60.

38 Ruth Battigheimer, *Grimms' Bad Girls and Bad Boys: The Moral and Social Vision of the Tales* (New Haven, CT, 1987), p. 160.

39 Volker, *The Animal in Far Eastern Art*, p. 7.

40 John M. Ellis, *One Fairy Story Too Many: The Brothers Grimm and their Tales* (Chicago, IL, 1983), p. 26.

3 THE LINGUISTIC FOX

1 T. Volker, *The Animal in Far Eastern Art, and Especially in the Art of the Japanese Netsuke, with References to Chinese Origins, Traditions,*

Legends and Art (Leiden, 1975), pp. 77–8.

2 Carmen Blacker, *The Catalpa Bow: A Study of Shamanistic Practices in Japan* (London, 1975), p. 51.

3 See Michael Bathgate, *The Fox's Craft in Japanese Religion and Folklore: Shapeshifters, Transformations and Duplicities* (New York, 2004), pp. 78–81.

4 For the Japanese fox terms, I have relied once again on Kiyoshi Nozaki, *Kitsunē: Japan's Fox of Mystery, Romance and Humor* (Tokyo, 1961), pp. 228–35.

5 For this information on the Irish Fox clan, I am endebted to the Sionnach Association Official Website maintained by M. J. Fox: www.geocities.com/foxclanirish/.

6 Ives Goddard, *Leonard Bloomfield's Fox Lexicon* (Winnipeg, 1994), p. 240.

7 Hugh F. Rankin, *Francis Marion: The Swamp Fox* (New York, 1973).

8 Quoted in Desmond Young, *Rommel: The Desert Fox* (New York, 1950), p. 7.

9 Miranda Green, *Animals in Celtic Life and Myth* (London, 1992), pp. 51–2.

10 Nozaki, *Kitsunē*, p. 181.

11 François Rabelais, *The Histories of Gargantua and Pantagruel*, trans. J. M. Cohen (Harmondsworth, 1955), Bk I, chap. XI.

12 Nozaki, *Kitsuné*, p. 121; Volker, *The Animal in Far Eastern Art*, p. 78.

13 *Aesop's Fables*, trans. V. S. Vernon (New York, 1912), p. 68.

14 Rabelais, *Gargantua and Pantagruel*, Bk I, chap. IX.

15 William Empson, *The Structure of Complex Words* (London, 1951), pp. 107, 110.

4 FOX-HUNTING

1 Keith Thomas, *Man and the Natural World: A History of the Modern Sensibility* (New York, 1983), p. 26.

2 Roger Scruton, *On Hunting* (London, 1998), p. 1n.

3 On the rise of animal rights, see Hilda Kean, *Animal Rights: Political and Social Change in Britain since 1800* (London, 1998); on

the double standard of the RSPCA, see Raymond Carr, *English Fox Hunting: A History* (London, 1976), pp. 198–204.

4 P. B. Munsche, *Gentlemen and Poachers: The English Game Laws, 1671–1831* (Cambridge, 1981), p. 3.

5 Stella A. Walker, *Sporting Art: England, 1700–1900* (New York, 1972), p. 13.

6 Fox-hunters began calling their prey Charlie as a slight to the Whig parliamentarian Charles James Fox, famous for, among other things, offering the toast 'Our Sovereign, the people', which won him the undying ire of Tory landholders.

7 This class distinction continues: the 10th Duke of Beaufort concludes his chapter on 'A Defence of Fox-Hunting' with the concession that 'human beings do have latent aggressive tendencies', and then asserts: 'better surely that those tendencies should be directed into a sport that is so exhilarating and carries with it goodwill and comradeship of the best kind, than that it should vent itself in soccer hooliganism and the sort of violence that makes the streets of our cities unsafe for both young and old' (Henry Hugh Arthur FitzRoy Somerset, Duke of Beaufort, *Fox Hunting*, London, 1980, p. 190).

8 Peter Beckford, *Thoughts on Hunting, in a Series of Familiar Letters to a Friend* (New York, 1926), pp. 148, 150 and 161.

9 Jane Ridley, *Fox Hunting* (London, 1990), p. 24; Carr, *English Fox Hunting*, p. 94; G. E. Mingay, *Land and Society in England, 1750–1980* (London, 1994), p. 131.

10 Martin Butlin and Evelyn Joll, eds, *The Paintings of J.M.W. Turner*, revd. edn (New Haven, CT, 1984), cat. 136n.

11 Walker, *Sporting Art*, p. 171.

12 Ridley, *Fox Hunting*, p. 51.

13 Anthony Trollope, *The Eustace Diamonds* (Oxford, 1983), pp. 352–3.

14 Siegfried Sassoon, *The Complete Memoirs of George Sherston* (London, 1937), p. 198.

15 Ibid., pp. 274 and 607.

16 Brian Vesey-Fitzgerald, *Town-Fox, Country Fox* (London, 1976), p. 88.

17 Charlie Pye-Smith, *Fox Hunting: Beyond the Propaganda* (Oakham,

Rutland, 1997), p. 25. The hunter's boast of conservation is as old as it is hollow. Keith Thomas cites a William Harrison, a sixteenth-century precursor to Mr Waldron, stating that foxes would have been 'utterly destroyed . . . many years agone' if they had not been protected by hunters (*Man and the Natural World*, p. 164).

18 Vesey-Fitzgerald, *Town-Fox*, p. 97.

19 Duke of Beaufort, *Fox Hunting*, p. 63.

20 Garry Marvin, 'Unspeakability, Inedibility and the Structures of Pursuit in the English Foxhunt', in *Representing Animals*, ed. Nigel Rothfels (Bloomington, IN, 2002), p. 145. See also Marvin, 'A Passionate Pursuit: Foxhunting as Performance', in *Nature Performed: Environment, Culture and Performance*, ed. Bronislaw Szerszynski, Wallace Heim and Clair Waterton (Oxford, 2003), pp. 46–60.

21 Vesey-Fitzgerald, *Town-Fox*, p. 17.

22 Donna Landry, *The Invention of the Countryside: Hunting, Walking and Ecology in English Literature, 1671–1831* (New York, 2001), p. 112.

5 THE COMMERCIAL FOX

1 Quoted in Raymond Carr, *English Fox Hunting: A History* (London, 1976), p.112.

2 Ibid, p. 111.

3 Lord Burns et al., *The Final Report of the Committee of Inquiry into Hunting with Dogs in England and Wales* (Norwich, 2000) p. 34.

4 Ibid., p. 35.

5 Michael Rosenthal, *The Art of Thomas Gainsborough: 'A Little Business for the Eye'* (New Haven, CT, 1999), p. 154.

6 Aileen Ribeiro, *Art of Dress: Fashion in England and France, 1750 to 1820* (New Haven, CT, 1995), p. 128.

7 Aileen Ribeiro, *Dress in Eighteenth-Century Europe* (New York, 1985), p. 147.

8 Ibid., p. 107.

9 Edgar Bailey, *Introduction of Foxes to Alaskan Islands: History, Effects on Avifauna, and Eradication*, United States Department of

the Interior Fish and Wildlife Service Resource Publication 193 (Washington, DC, 1993), p. 3.

10 Joseph Forester and Anne D. Forester, *Silver Fox Odyssey: History, of the Canadian Silver Fox Industry* (Prince Edward Island, n. d.), p. 6.

11 According to Animal Aid: *www.animalaid.org.uk*

12 Forester and Forester, *Silver Fox Odyssey*, p. 28.

13 From the IFTF website: *www.iftf.com/farming.asp*

14 Bailey, *Introduction of Foxes to Alaskan Islands*, p. 2.

15 Forrester and Forrester, *Silver Fox Odyssey*, p. 73.

16 www.iftf.com/farming.asp

17 Julia V. Emberley, *The Cultural Politics of Fur* (Ithaca, NY, 1997), p. 3.

18 Ibid., pp. 192–203.

19 Jorge Crespo, 'Ecology of the Pampas Gray Fox and the Large Fox (*Culpeo*)', in *The Wild Canids: Their Systematics, Behavioral Ecology and Evolution*, ed. M. W. Fox (New York, 1975), p. 188; according to Crespo, the *culpeo* is the second largest canid in South America.

20 Frederick E. Zeuner, *A History of Domesticated Animals* (New York, 1963), p. 424.

21 Ibid.

22 Yi-Fu Tuan, *Dominance and Affection: The Making of Pets* (New Haven, CT, 1984), p. 90.

23 George F. Lyon, *Private Journal*, 1824; quoted in E. T. Seton, *Lives of Game Animals* (Boston, MA, 1953), vol. I, part 2, p. 449.

24 Reay Tannahill, *Food in History* (New York, 1973), p. 214.

25 Tuan, *Dominance and Affection*, p. 77.

26 Zeuner, *A History of Domesticated Animals*, p. 417.

27 Knut Schmidt-Nielson, *Desert Animals: Physiological Problems of Heat and Water* (Oxford, 1964), p. 126.

28 Ibid., p. 127.

29 David Macdonald, *Running with the Fox* (New York, 1987), p. 56.

30 Seton, *Lives of Game Animals*, vol. I, part 2, pp. 589–90.

31 Louise E. Robbins, *Elephant Slaves and Pampered Parrots: Exotic Animals in Eighteenth-Century Paris* (Baltimore, MD, 2002), pp. 145, 152.

6 TWENTIETH-CENTURY FOX: THE CINEMA

1 These quotations are from the novel on which the film is based, and whose dialogue is retained closely in the film: Mary Webb, *Gone to Earth* (London, 1932), p. 33.

2 Ibid., p. 67.

3 Ibid.

4 Ibid., p. 176.

5 Ibid., p. 63.

6 Ibid., p. 88.

7 Rania Huntington, *Alien Kind: Foxes and Late Chinese Narrative* (Cambridge, MA, 2003), p. 184.

8 Ibid., pp. 171 and 178.

Bibliography

Aesop's Fables, trans. V. S. Vernon (New York, 1912)

Ables, E. D., 'Ecology of the Red Fox in North America', in *The Wild Canids: Their Systematics, Behavioral Ecology and Evolution*, ed. M. W. Fox (New York, 1975), pp. 216–36

Apollodorus, *The Library*, trans. Sir James George Frazer (Cambridge, MA, 1921)

Aristotle, *History of Animals*, trans. A. L. Peck (Cambridge, MA, 1965)

—, *On the Soul; Parva Naturalia, On Breath*, trans. W. S. Hett (Cambridge, MA, 1975)

Bailey, Edgar, *Introduction of Foxes to Alaskan Islands: History, Effects of Avifauna and Eradication*, United States Department of the Interior Fish and Wildlife Service Resource Publication 193 (Washington, DC, 1993)

Baird, Spencer Fullerton, *Mammals of North America* (Philadelphia, PA, 1857)

Bathgate, Michael, *The Fox's Craft in Japanese Religion and Folklore: Shapeshifters, Transformations and Duplicities* (New York, 2004)

Battigheimer, Ruth, *Grimms' Bad Girls and Bad Boys: The Moral and Social Vision of the Tales* (New Haven, CT, 1987)

Beaufort, Henry Hugh Arthur FitzRoy Somerset, Duke of, *Fox Hunting* (London, 1980)

Beckford, Peter, *Thoughts on Hunting, in a Series of Familiar Letters to a Friend* (New York, 1926)

Bindman, David, *Ape to Apollo: Aesthetics and the Idea of Race in the Eighteenth Century* (Ithaca, NY, 2002)

Blacker, Carmen, *The Catalpa Bow: A Study of Shamanistic Practices in*

Japan (London, 1975)

Block, Elaine C., and Kenneth Varty, 'Choir-Stall Carvings of Reynard and Other Foxes', in *Reynard the Fox: Social Engagement and Cultural Metamorphoses in the Beast Epic from the Middle Ages to the Present*, ed. Kenneth Varty (New York, 2000), pp. 125–62

Buffon, George-Louis Leclerc, Comte de, *Selections from Natural History, General and Particular*, 4 vols (New York, 1977)

Burns, Lord, et al., *The Final Report of the Committee of Inquiry into Hunting with Dogs in England and Wales* (Norwich, 2000)

Butlin, Martin, and Evelyn Joll, eds, *The Paintings of J.M.W. Turner*, revd edn (New Haven, CT, 1984)

Carlill, James, trans., *The Epic of the Beast, Consisting of Translations of The History of Raynard the Fox and Physiologus* (London, n. d.)

Carr, Raymond, *English Fox Hunting: A History* (London, 1976)

Chan, Leo Tak-hung, *The Discourse on Foxes and Ghosts: Ji Yun and Eighteenth-Century Literati Storytelling* (Honolulu, HI, 1998)

Chesemore, David L., 'Ecology of the Arctic Fox', in *The Wild Canids: Their Systematics, Behavioral Ecology and Evolution*, ed. M. W. Fox (New York, 1975), pp. 143–63

Crespo, Jorge A., 'Ecology of the Pampas Gray Fox and the Large Fox (Culpeo)', in *The Wild Canids: Their Systematics, Behavioral Ecology and Evolution*, ed. M. W. Fox (New York, 1975), pp. 179–91

Darwin, Charles, *Voyage of the Beagle* (New York, 1909)

Eliade, Mircea, *Shamanism: Archaic Techniques of Ecstasy*, trans. Willard R. Trask (New York, 1964)

Ellis, John M., *One Fairy Story Too Many: The Brothers Grimm and their Tales* (Chicago, IL, 1983)

Emberley, Julia V., *The Cultural Politics of Fur* (Ithaca, NY, 1997)

Empson, William, *The Structure of Complex Words* (London, 1951)

Evans, E. P., *Animal Symbolism in Ecclesiastical Architecture* (London, 1896)

Faraci, Dora, 'The Bestiary and its Sources: Some Examples', *Reinardus: Yearbook of the International Reynard Society*, VII (1994), pp. 31–43

Forester, Joseph, and Anne D. Forester, *Silver Fox Odyssey: History of the Canadian Silver Fox Industry* (Prince Edward Island, n. d.)

Fox, M. W., ed., *The Wild Canids: Their Systematics, Behavioral Ecology and Evolution* (New York, 1975)

Frazer, Sir James, *The Golden Bough: A Study in Magic and Religion* (New York, 1922)

French, Roger, *Ancient Natural History: Histories of Nature* (London, 1994)

Goddard, Ives, *Leonard Bloomfield's Fox Lexicon* (Winnipeg, 1994)

Grambo, Rebecca, *The World of the Fox* (San Francisco, CA, 1995)

Green, Miranda, *Animals in Celtic Life and Myth* (London, 1992)

Hawhee, Debra, *Bodily Arts: Rhetoric and Athletics in Ancient Greece* (Austin, TX, 2004)

Henry, J. David, *Red Fox: The Catlike Canine* (Washington, DC, 1996)

Howe, James, 'Fox Hunting as Ritual', *American Ethnologist*, VIII (1981), pp. 278–300

Kean, Hilda, *Animal Rights: Political and Social Change in Britain since 1800* (London, 1998)

Kurtén, Björn, *Pleistocene Mammals of Europe* (London, 1968)

—, and Elain Anderson, *Pleistocene Mammals of North America* (New York, 1980)

Landry, Donna, *The Invention of the Countryside: Hunting, Walking and Ecology in English Literature, 1671–1831* (New York, 2001)

Langguth, Alfredo, 'Ecology and Evolution in the South American Canids', in *The Wild Canids: Their Systematics, Behavioral Ecology and Evolution*, ed. M. W. Fox (New York, 1975), pp. 192–215

Lloyd, Huw Glen, 'The Red Fox in Britain', in *The Wild Canids: Their Systematics, Behavioral Ecology and Evolution*, ed. M. W. Fox (New York, 1975), pp. 207–15

Macdonald, David, *Running with the Fox* (New York, 1987)

Marvin, Garry, 'A Passionate Pursuit: Foxhunting as Performance', in *Nature Performed: Environment, Culture and Performance*, ed. Bronislaw Szerszynski, Wallace Heim and Claire Waterton (Oxford, 2003)

—, 'Unspeakability, Inedibility and the Structures of Pursuit in the English Foxhunt', in *Representing Animals*, ed. Nigel Rothfels

(Bloomington, IN, 2002)

Merrifield, Ralph, *The Archaeology of Ritual and Magic* (New York, 1987)

Mingay, G. E., *Land and Society in England, 1750–1980* (London, 1994)

Munsche, P. B., *Gentlemen and Poachers: The English Game Laws, 1671–1831* (Cambridge, 1981)

Nozaki, Kiyoshi, *Kitsunē: Japan's Fox of Mystery, Romance and Humor* (Tokyo, 1961)

Parker, R. B., '*Volpone* and *Reynard the Fox*', *Renaissance Drama*, VII (1977), pp. 3–42

Pausanius, *Description of Greece*, trans. W.H.S. Jones (Cambridge, MA, 1918)

Plato, *Sophist*, trans. Harold North Fowler (Cambridge, MA, 1987)

Pliny the Elder, *Natural History*, trans. H. Rackham (Cambridge, MA, 1961)

Pye-Smith, Charlie, *Fox Hunting: Beyond the Propaganda* (Oakham, Rutland, 1997)

Rankin, Hugh F., *Francis Marion: The Swamp Fox* (New York, 1973)

Ribeiro, Aileen, *Art of Dress: Fashion in England and France, 1750 to 1820* (New Haven, CT, 1995)

—, *Dress in Eighteenth-Century Europe* (New York, 1985)

Ridley, Jane, *Fox Hunting* (London, 1990)

Robbins, Louise E., *Elephant Slaves and Pampered Parrots: Exotic Animals in Eighteenth-Century Paris* (Baltimore, MD, 2002)

Rosenthal, Michael, *The Art of Thomas Gainsborough: 'A Little Business for the Eye'* (New Haven, CT, 1999)

Rosevear, D. R., *The Carnivores of West Africa* (London, 1974)

Ross, Anne, 'Lindow Man and the Celtic Tradition', in *Lindow Man: The Body in the Bog*, ed. I. M. Stead, J. B. Bourke and Don Brothwell (London, 1986), pp. 162–9

—, *The Pagan Celts* (Totowa, NJ, 1986)

Rowland, Beryl, *Animals with Human Faces: A Guide to Animal Symbolism* (Knoxville, TN, 1973)

Rüppel, von G., 'A "Lie" as a Directed Message of the Arctic Fox (*Alopex lagopus L.*)', in *Deception: Perspectives on Human and*

Nonhuman Deceit, ed. Robert W. Mitchell and Nicholas S. Thompson (Albany, NY, 1982), pp. 177–81

Sands, Donald B., ed., *The History of Reynard the Fox, Translated and Printed by William Caxton in 1481* (Cambridge, MA, 1960)

Sappho, *Greek Lyric*, trans. David A. Campbell (Cambridge, MA, 1982)

Sassoon, Siegfried, *The Complete Memoirs of George Sherston* (London, 1937)

Schmidt-Nielson, Knut, *Desert Animals: Physiological Problems of Heat and Water* (Oxford, 1964)

Scruton, Roger, *On Hunting* (London, 1998)

Seton, E. T., *Lives of Game Animals* (Boston, MA, 1953)

Sheldon, Jennifer, *Wild Dogs: The Natural History of the Nondomestic Canidae* (New York, 1992)

Smith, K., 'The Excavation of Winklebury Camp, Basingstoke, Hampshire', *Proceedings of the Prehistorical Society*, XLIII (1977), pp. 31–129

Stains, Howard J., 'Distribution and Taxonomy of the Canidae', in *The Wild Canids: Their Systematics, Behavioral Ecology and Evolution*, ed. M. W. Fox (New York, 1975), pp. 3–26

Stead, I. M., J. B. Bourke and Don Brotherwell, eds, *Lindow Man: The Body in the Bog* (London, 1986)

Stephenson, Roger, 'The Political Import of Goethe's *Reineke Fuchs*', in *Reynard the Fox: Social Engagement and Cultural Metamorphoses in the Beast Epic from the Middle Ages to the Present*, ed. Kenneth Varty (New York, 2000), pp. 191–207

Tannahill, Reay, *Food in History* (New York, 1973)

Thomas, Keith, *Man and the Natural World: A History of the Modern Sensibility* (New York, 1983)

Trapp, Gene R., and Donald L. Hallberg, 'Ecology of the Gray Fox (*Urocyon cinereoargenteus*): A Review', in *The Wild Canids: Their Systematics, Behavioral Ecology and Evolution*, ed. M. W. Fox (New York, 1975), pp. 164–78

Trollope, Anthony, *The Eustace Diamonds* (Oxford, 1983)

Tuan, Yi-Fu, *Dominance and Affection: The Making of Pets* (New Haven, CT, 1984)

Urton, Gary, 'Animal Metaphors and the Life Cycle in an Andean Community', in his *Animal Myths and Metaphors in South America* (Salt Lake City, UT, 1985), pp. 251–84

—, ed., *Animal Myths and Metaphors in South America* (Salt Lake City, UT, 1985)

Varty, Kenneth, *Reynard, Renart, Reinaert and Other Foxes in Medieval England: The Iconographic Evidence* (Amsterdam, 1999)

—, ed., *Reynard the Fox: Social Engagement and Cultural Metamorphoses in the Beast Epic from the Middle Ages to the Present* (New York, 2000)

—, and Jean Dufournet, 'The Death and Resurrection of the *Roman de Renart*', in *Reynard the Fox: Social Engagement and Cultural Metamorphoses in the Beast Epic from the Middle Ages to the Present*, ed. Kenneth Varty (New York, 2000), pp. 221–44

Vesey-Fitzgerald, Brian, *Town-Fox, Country Fox* (London, 1976)

Volker, T., *The Animal in Far Eastern Art, and Especially in the Art of the Japanese Netsuke, with References to Chinese Origins, Traditions, Legends and Art* (Leiden, 1975)

Wade, Clyde, 'Reynard and Volpone: The Expanding Analogy', *Publications of the Missouri Philological Association*, II (1977), pp. 24–32

Walker, Stella A., *Sporting Art: England, 1700–1900* (New York, 1972)

Webb, Mary, *Gone to Earth* (London, 1932)

Young, Desmond, *Rommel: The Desert Fox* (New York, 1950)

Zeuner, Frederick E., *A History of Domesticated Animals* (New York, 1963)

Zimen, Erik, ed., *The Red Fox: Symposium on Behaviour and Ecology* (The Hague, 1980)

Zuidema, R. Tom, 'The Lion in the City: Royal Symbols of Transition in Cuzco', in *Animal Myths and Metaphors in South America*, ed. Gary Urton (Salt Lake City, UT, 1985), pp. 183–250

Associations and Websites

CANID SPECIALIST GROUP

www.canids.org

A branch of the World Conservation Union (www.iucn.org), this
group of scientists, photographers and naturalists focuses on the
biology and conservation of canids worldwide. The website has
some lovely photographs of rare fox species.

Dr Claudio Sillero-Zubiri

Wildlife Conservation Research Unit

Oxford University

Tubney House, Abington Road

Tubney OX13 5QL

www.academia-issendai.com/fox-index.shtml

This is a prime resource for information on Asian fox-spirits, with
detailed information on Chinese, Japanese and Korean stories,
with a solid bibliography of books – scholarly and popular – and
films dealing with fox-spirits.

www.foxes-online.com

This site lists films and TV shows dealing with foxes.

THE FOX CLAN

www.geocities.com/foxclanirish/foxindex.html

This website, managed by the Sionnach clan, is continually
updated with information on the history of Fox families and clans
throughout the world. The site also provides photographs of

places in Ireland associated with the clan and the means to explore family connections.

HIDDEN: THE OFFICIAL ARCTIC FOX FANLISTING
www.spring-breeze.net/hidden/
> This organization provides access for admirers of the Arctic fox around the world.

INTERNATIONAL REYNARD SOCIETY
www.welcometo/tiecelijn
> This organization was founded by the inestimable Professor Kenneth Varty in 1975 to further the study of Beast Epic, Fable and Fabliau. It publishes the annual journal *Reinardus*, which presents the current scholarly research on Reynardiana. An affiliated review, in Dutch, is *Tiecelijn*, edited by Rik van Daele.

Kitsune.org
> This site (not to be confused with the plethora of sites promoting the video game of this name) is probably the richest compendium of Asian tales of foxes.

MASTER OF FOX HOUNDS ASSOCIATION (MFHA)
www.mfha.co.uk
> The primary source for information on hunting in the UK.
> The Old School
> Bagendon
> Cirencester, Gloucestershire GL7 7DU

MASTER OF FOX HOUNDS ASSOCIATION OF NORTH AMERICA
www.mfha.com
> The primary source for information on hunting in the United States.
> PO Box 363
> Millwood, Virginia 22626, USA

NATIONAL FOX WELFARE SOCIETY

http://www.nfws.org.uk

This society provides advice concerning foxes suffering from Sarcoptic mange.

135 Higham Road

Rushden, Northants, NN10 6DS

REINEKE FUCHS MUSEUM

www.reinekefuchsmuseum.org

This museum includes a wide array of artefacts, images and information on the medieval tales of the rogue Reineke, as well as material on foxes more generally.

Reineke-Fuchs Museum

Dresdener Strasse 22

35440 Linden-Leihgestern

Germany

SEFALO

www.zoologi.su.se/research/alopex/homesefalo.html

The Swedish-Finnish-Norwegian Arctic Fox Project is a five-year programme (2003–8) aimed at preserving the Arctic fox and its habitat from incursions by humans and other predators, particularly the red fox.

Dr Anders Angerbjörn

Department of Zoology

Stockholm University

SE-106 91 Stockholm, Sweden

www.urbanfoxes.org

This site, which focuses on American urban foxes, is maintained by a vulpephile, T. Susman. Its aim is to complement studies in Britain by David Macdonald and others. It also provides links to other fox websites.

Acknowledgements

One of the joys of writing about foxes has been learning that almost everyone has a story of their own about an encounter with adorable kits, fleet-footed vixens, or thieving stinking vermin, and in hearing these tales I have had to learn just how varied the cultural and personal views of foxes are. The off-hand comment as much as the serious discursus has challenged my thinking about foxes – and animals generally – in surprising and new ways. To all those who have described their vulpine sightings, told me their foxy joke, or simply raised questions I had not thought of, I give my thanks.

Many people have also given me more specific help in such matters as locating paintings or photographs, finding poems, and letting me know about important details I would have otherwise neglected. Jonathan Burt provided invaluable guidance from the beginning. Anne Dunan worked overtime negotiating with French authorities. My mate from Tooting, Kevin Jackson, D. G., told me about Foucault's nickname, Char, and the Spartan who was eaten by a fox. Alec Jackson and Garry Marvin each suggested rich sources on hunting. Jody Nicotra helped deepen my conception of *metis*. Christopher Page, who married a fox, once again facilitated the way through Cambridge, despite my tardiness at breakfast. Claire Preston listened patiently to my rants, and introduced me to the easeful life of Damariscotta. Kenneth Varty generously aided my search for medieval foxes. Linda Austin has never once told me to stop going on about the 21 species.

Financial assistance came from Carol Moder, head of my home department, who provided the means for me to travel to England and France in search of carvings depicting the ancient sport of bibulism.

The Oklahoma Humanities Council generously contributed funds to meet some of the exorbitant reproduction fees charged by museums and galleries.

Hugh Manon helped with major photographic tasks. Elsa Foley, Charissa Prchal and Jenneffer Sixkiller patiently lent their expertise, and never complained when I lost their work and had to ask them again. My thanks to the staff at Reaktion, especially Harry Gilonis, who made what seemed an insurmountable and tedious task into an unexpected joy.

Finally, I wish to thank my parents for their constant encouragement and support. It is to them and Otto M. Austin that I wish to dedicate this book.

Photo Acknowledgements

The author and publishers wish to express their thanks to the below sources of illustrative material and/or permission to reproduce it. (Some sources uncredited in the captions for reasons of brevity are also given below.)

Photo by Daryl Abbot/SWREF: p. 19; Archives de la Galerie Brame et Lorenceau, Paris: p. 14; photo by the author: p. 87; from Spencer Fullerton Baird, *Mammals of North America* (Philadelphia, 1859): p. 18; photo Florian Batschi / ftcb.de [ftcb/Flickr] p. 38; British Library, London (Ms Roy. B VII): p. 45; photo © Burnand/Roger-Viollet (BUR-5852), courtesy of Rex Features: p. 120; photo Courtauld Institute of Art, London: p. 99; photo Mary McCartney Donald, courtesy of PETA: p. 140; photo David Eppstein [OXDE/Flickr]: p. 25; photo Fine Art Photographic Library, London / Art Resource, NY: p. 110; photo Fitzwilliam Museum, University of Cambridge: p. 95; photos Elsa Foley: pp. 16, 26, 44, 53, 55, 61, 62, 64 (top), 66, 76, 77, 80, 106, 119, 168; photo Dennis Glennon: p. 32; Iveagh Bequest, Kenwood: p. 98; photos Jaime Jimenez: p. 22 (foot). 27, 34 (top); photo Jeff Le Clere: p. 75; photos The Library of Congress, Washington, DC: pp. 40 (Prints and Photographs Division, LC-USZC4-10063), 79 (Prints and Photographs Division, LC-USZC4-3411), 133 (LC-USZ62-99603), 145 (Prints and Photographs Division, LC-USF33-016019-M1); photos Hugh Manon: pp. 64 (foot), 65, 71, 122; The Metropolitan Museum of Art, New York (bequest of Edward S. Harkness, 1940 [50.135.5]), photo The Metropolitan Museum of Art, all rights reserved: p. 128; photo courtesy of the artist (William Morris): p. 57; Musée de Chantilly, Condé: p. 97; National Gallery, London (NG 683), photo National Gallery: p. 127; photo John Newby/Sahara Conservation Fund: p. 31; photos *Paris-Match*, 23 November 1963: p. 13; photos Rex Features: pp. 12 (Richard Austin/Rex Features, 505168E), 34

Index